Shepherd
my

A Study of the 23rd Psalm

Advantage™
INSPIRATIONAL

Frankie Lee, Th.D.

My Shepherd: A Study of the 23rd Psalm by Frankie Lee
Copyright © 2008 by Curtis F. Lee
All Rights Reserved.
ISBN: 1-59755-136-8

Published by: ADVANTAGE BOOKS™
www.advbookstore.com

Unless otherwise indicated, Bible quotations are taken from the King James Version of the Bible.

Library of Congress Control Number: 2008930351

Cover design by Pat Theriault

First Printing: July 2008
08 09 10 11 12 13 14   10 9 8 7 6 5 4 3 2 1
Printed in the United States of America

Dedicated To The Memory of

Miss Alice Woods
and
Dr. Avery Rogers

"Who Dwell In The Lord's House"

Curtiss F. Lee, TH. B., TH. D.

Introduction

This is not a study that takes liberty with God's Word in the King James Bible. I am not an apologist for God's Word. His Word speaks for itself. My purpose is not to discuss the doctrines of the church or any particular belief system. Rather, this is a treatise on the relationship between the Shepherd and His sheep.

I keep these words from C. H. Spurgeon in the front of my Bible:

"Either this book is true from cover to cover, or it is not worth one solitary penny to me. It may be to a man who is so wise to distinguish between a truth or an error but I am such a fool I cannot do that. "

Instead of expounding on what God's Word is trying to tell or what it says or means I have let it speak for itself. I have used over three hundred direct quotations from the King James Version of the Bible, from over forty-five of the sixty-six books. This was Jesus' method during his earthly ministry. He quoted from the Scripture available to Him, "It is written". Since the psalmist, David, writing the twenty-third Psalm wrote "The Lord is", I have in my writing included only a portion of an unexplainable Lord's attributes. The Scripture uses a form of the term "The Lord is" to identify Him and His attributes over fifty-three times in some fashion. I'm listing them here without specific scripture reference, but you will recognize most of them.

The Lord is righteous, my strength, a man of war, with us, long suffering, God, your way, a God of knowledge, witness, my rock, able, king, my shepherd, my light, good, our defense, The Lord; my refuge, upright, clothed with strength, great, merciful and gracious, on my side, my keeper, nigh, far from the wicked, the maker, the Lord Jehovah, everlasting, a God of judgment, exalted, our judge, our lawgiver, our king, the Lord the redeemer, the Lord thy redeemer, risen, the true God, there, the Lord, the God of hosts, slow to anger, a consuming fire, Jesus Christ, at hand, the avenger, fateful, my helper, very pitiful, gracious, not slack, my salvation, and He is the Lord of Lords and the King of Kings.

This book has its origin in extemporaneous lectures of Dr. Avery Rogers given in 1974, which I recorded. To these I have added notes from studies and lectures from many sources I have compiled over thirty-five years. Most notable are from writings of C. H. Spurgeon called "explanatory notes and quaint sayings" of writers of his day and before that, which are found at the end of each Psalm in his writings.

The knowledge of sheep and the shepherd's life that I have was increased greatly by those descriptions of pastoral life in Palestine. I have endeavored to put this knowledge in a simple form that anyone with an inquisitive mind can understand, mostly in conversational language. I trust that the reader will have a more in-depth understanding of the twenty-third Psalm after reading this study. If it helps but one soul, my goal has been accomplished.

The first thing to die in Scripture was a lamb. The first man to die was a shepherd. The first to be told of the Savior's birth in Scripture were shepherds. The first man to die without sin was the Lamb of God, Jesus. It was only fitting that the first to rise from the dead would be the Lamb of God, Jesus, the Good Shepherd, my Shepherd.

May God bless all who read this work.

Table of Contents

Chapter One

THE SHEPHERD-HOOD
OF THE SAVIOR

"The Lord Is"

The Lord is my shepherd. I shall not want. He maketh me to lie down in green pastures. He leadeth me beside the still waters. He restoreth my soul. He leadeth me in the paths of righteousness for his name's sake. Yea, though I walk through the valley of the shadow of death, I will fear no evil, for thou art with me. Thy rod and thy staff they comfort me. Thou preparest a table before me in the presence of mine enemies; thou anointest my head with oil. My cup runneth over. Surely, goodness and mercy shall follow me all the days of my life and I shall dwell in the house of the Lord forever. (Psalm 23)

I am the good shepherd. The good shepherd giveth his life for the sheep. John 10:11

I am always referring to the Lord Jesus Christ as the Shepherd. Numerous descriptions of the Lord Jesus Christ show that this is an excellent metaphor. He is the one that paid for our sin, and that is where salvation ends. I want to present what the Shepherd does and is in this study. The shepherd-hood of the Savior as found in the Scripture will be discussed in this chapter.

First I want to mention that sheep are mentioned in the Bible, as near as I can count, 192 times. In the Old Testament they are mentioned 154 times, and in the New Testament 38 times. Lamb is mentioned 164 times, 131 times in the Old Testament, 33 times in the New.

The word shepherd is found in the Bible approximately 83 times: 65 in the Old Testament, 18 in the New. All these references to shepherd and sheep are related to the Holy Land, and they are all favorable, not one crude or out of order. The shepherd and his sheep are always in right relationship with each other. It is always orderly right down the line, correct. So when we study shepherd and sheep in the Bible, we are reading something that has been recorded in such fine order that those who would criticize it have not found any mistakes or anything inaccurate in it.

Sheep are willing to die. You can cut one's throat and bleed it -- draw blood out and it will not resist, will not bleat, will not kick back, just accept it as if saying, "All right, I will let you do it." You can cut its wool off and sometimes nick its skin; it will just lie there, willing to die, willing to give up its wool. There are no crude statements in the Bible about the shepherd and the sheep. If you hear contradictory stories from other sources, do not believe them. Nowhere in the world do the shepherd and the sheep compare to those in the Holy Land. They are entirely different. The subject of the shepherd and his sheep has been largely neglected by writers and ministers since The Treasury of David was written by C. H. Spurgeon prior to 1892. So I have decided to revisit the subject of the shepherd and sheep, as it is presented in the Bible.

Jesus Christ is presented in the Bible as a shepherd. He is presented in His shepherd-hood, and it is a three-fold shepherd-hood. He is called the Good Shepherd, the Great Shepherd and the Chief Shepherd. All the references made to him throughout; all the ways in which the shepherd-hood of Jesus Christ are recorded, have scriptural and spiritual significance. Therefore, I will attempt to present in this book, the Shepherd in his three-fold shepherd-hood. "The Lord is my shepherd." He has shepherd-hood. The Lord in the 23rd Psalm is Jesus Christ.

I. THE GOOD SHEPHERD

Jesus Christ is, first of all, the Good Shepherd. The Good Shepherd saves us from the penalty for sin. Notice what John 10:11 says: the Good Shepherd gives his life for the sheep. He saves the sheep from the penalty of sin. The penalty for sin is always death. " . . . the wages of sin is death" (Romans 6:23). And it is a three-fold death.

It is spiritual death, then physical death, and then eternal death. Remember when God said to Adam , " . . . in the day that thou eatest thereof thou shalt surely die" (Genesis 2:17). People have argued that this cannot be true because he and Eve did not die that day. What they were thinking about is that they did not die <u>physically</u> that day, and that much is true. They did not die physically that day. They died spiritually that day. Death in the Bible means separation. When Adam and Eve sinned, they separated themselves from God. They ran from God, hid from God. They died spiritually that day. The spiritual life they had died.

When God said, you shall die, that also referred to the physical death. Adam and Eve did die physically later on. Every man since then has died, except for Enoch and Elijah. I believe they are the two witnesses who will return and then die during the tribulation period (Revelation 11:3-12).

Sin produces spiritual death and after that, physical death. When I die physically there is a separation that will take place. My spirit will be separated from my body. James said that, "the body without the Spirit is dead (James 2:26)". There is a physical separation when death comes.

Then, if you are lost and die without Jesus Christ as your Savior, you will die the eternal death. That is death in the lake of fire and brimstone, which is called in Revelation "the second death." That death is eternal. It means existing without God forever in hell, and there is no remedy for it.

When Christ came as the Good Shepherd, He went to the cross for us and died to pay the three-fold penalty. He died to save us from spiritual death. He died to save us from physical death because, if you are born again, you will be resurrected, and he died to save us from eternal death.

As the Good Shepherd, and He was a good one, in that He loved us enough to die for us and to give Himself for the penalty of sin that had been passed on to us from Adam, He paid the penalty Himself. He took the penalty we should have paid for our sin upon Himself.

No person is able to save himself from the penalty of sin. It takes Jesus Christ. Unless you accept Him, you will never be saved from the penalty of sin. Jesus Christ as the Good Shepherd came and gave His life for the sheep. God will not require the penalty for sin to be paid twice.

If you accept Jesus Christ as your Lord and Savior, you will never die spiritually. If you accept Jesus Christ as your Savior, you can rest assured that the Good Shepherd has saved you from the penalty of sin, and you will never have to endure that penalty. You will never receive the judgment that God renders upon the lost for their sin.

Jesus Christ voluntarily paid that penalty for us. He said, "No man taketh it (my life) from me, but I lay it down of myself. I have power to lay it down and I have power to take it again . . . ". God gave it to Him, and Jesus voluntarily paid the penalty price for our sin on Calvary. That is why He is called the Good Shepherd. Anyone who would love you like that, to bear the penalty for your sin, and face the hell of death that He did, has to be good, and He is. He is the Good Shepherd.

While I am here, I have to tell you that Psalm 22, as well as the Psalm 23, tells us much about the Good Shepherd. Psalm 22 is about how the Good Shepherd dies; it is a prophecy of the Good Shepherd. It tells us Jesus Christ will come and die for us.

II. THE GREAT SHEPHERD

Not only is Jesus called the Good Shepherd in scripture, He also is called the Great Shepherd. The 23rd Psalm talks about what He does for us as the Great Shepherd.

Jesus is called The Great Shepherd in the New Testament in Hebrews 13:20-21. "Now the God of peace, that brought again from the dead our Lord Jesus, that great shepherd of the sheep, through the blood of the everlasting covenant, Make you perfect in every good work to do his will, working in you that which is well pleasing in his sight, through Jesus Christ . . ."

Psalm 23 is a prophecy of Jesus Christ as the Great Shepherd; Palm 22 as the Good Shepherd. Sin not only has a penalty; sin has power. The Great Shepherd has to save us from the power of sin. He died as the Good Shepherd to save us from the penalty of sin, and He lives as the Great Shepherd to save us from the power of sin. He keeps sin from dominating our lives. No man has the strength in himself to overcome the power of sin in his life, but the power of Jesus working through us makes us overcomers.

How is a man able to escape the power of sin? It cannot be from eradication. I mean by that, when God saves you, He does not remove your sin nature. He does not pull it out; you still have it.

The Apostle Paul had been a Christian for 20 years when he said in Romans 7:18, "I know that in me (that is in my flesh) dwelleth no good thing . . . " And in Romans 7:24 he said, "O wretched man that I am! Who shall deliver me from the body of this death?" So you did not get rid of the old sin nature when you were saved. You still have it. You carry it around with you. You will never get rid of it for the rest of this life, in this world. But in the life to come you will. You have to combat your sinful nature every day. You do not have any power over sin of yourself. You cannot get rid of the power of sin by eradication.

Neither do we overcome sin by suppression. There are folks who say, "Oh, I am going to do better. I am just going to suppress this thing. I am not going to let it control me any longer. I am going to quit abusing my body. I am going to quit thinking only of myself. I am going to quit eating wrong." But they don't. They can keep the lid on their sinful nature for a little while but then it will blow off. You can say you are not going to do this, that or the other thing. But you do not get delivered from the power of sin by suppressing those evil, sinful, tainted desires in your life.

Neither do you get rid of them by counter activities that are supposed to divert your attention. All the programs to keep people busy make no difference. You know what some are trying to do? They're trying to give young people lots of entertainment. "If we give them this, that, or the other, they will not do wrong." Well, do not kid yourself. Do not kid them. The trouble is not around us, but in us.

In the spring of 1975 I wrote a letter to Miss Alice Moore, the lady to whom I co-dedicated this book, about a meeting conducted by the other person I dedicated this book to, Dr. Avery Rogers. In her reply to me, Miss Moore wrote, "Only the Lord knows how much I would have loved to be in that revival in your church; to have been a part of the good old time Gospel preaching, that good old time 73 year old preacher (Dr. Avery Rogers), called and put in the pulpit by God himself, would do. Frankie, I need that kind of preaching. There is so little of it being done now, but rather a lot of all night singing, ball games, sweetheart parties, food and drink all in the House of the Lord - and the people sit by - and let it happen and tolerate it. Don't you know the Lord does not approve of that kind of stuff in his house?"

This lady was a single person in her seventies, a dear saint of God who went to the Lord's House to dwell forever in the early 1980s. This letter was written to me on Feb. 19, 1975. Can you imagine her assessment of the things taking place in the Lord's House today? You know what we are trying to do in this day and time? We are trying to sanctify sin. You can not sanctify sin, not even if you do it in the name of the church. We are sinful, and unable to liberate ourselves from sin because somebody has to do it <u>for us,</u> and the One that does is Jesus Christ. You will have to be liberated from sin by His power alone. He delivers you from the power of sin by transforming you.

Look again at Hebrews 13:20 & 21. "that great shepherd . . . Make you perfect in every good work to do his will, working in you that which is wellpleasing in his sight, through Jesus Christ . . ." He puts His Spirit in you, to give you power over sin. He that is in you is greater than he that is in the world. The Great Shepherd delivers you from the power of sin. That is why Psalm 23 says, "The Lord is my shepherd." The Lord has all power. (I will discuss the names and the power contained in the names of God that are included in this name, Lord, in a later chapter.)

He can transform you alive, and cause you to live by His power, like God wants you to. He liberates you from the power of sin and enables you to live a righteous life. He enables you to do God's will. He enables you to do that which is wellpleasing to God. That is what this scripture says. He transforms you so you can do the work of God, and say that you please God in your walk, in your daily life.

There are some people who say they cannot hold out. "I would like to be a Christian, but I do not think I can hold out." In your journey, you are going to fall. If you walk by yourself, you will never get there. It takes someone greater than you and I. Jesus Christ has come as the Great Shepherd, and He can hold out. He can hold us and hold out too. Do you understand how the Great Shepherd relationship works? He has the power. He delivers us by His power and causes us to do the will of God, the work of God, and to be more pleasing in God's sight.

Sin lies in its power to give pleasure. People sin because they love it. It pleases them. I am not going to say that sin is not pleasurable to a sinner. There is pleasure in it. Sin has pleasure for the lost man. He likes it. He revels in it and it is a real thrill to him. All sin has pleasure, at least at the beginning.

But Jesus Christ comes into your life and gives you a life that has pleasure in Him. If a person really knows the pleasure of a relationship with the Lord Jesus Christ, sin has no power over him. The Word of God it says, " . . . in thy presence is fulness of joy, at thy right hand there are pleasures for evermore" (Psalm 16:11). There is more pleasure with Christ Jesus in one split second than in all the pleasures of sin for a lifetime.

You may feel you have to run somewhere to get pleasure to satisfy yourself because there is something on the inside of you that is hunkered down and cannot be still. There is not something wrong with Jesus, it is wrong with you. You are in a bad way. If you need the television on all the time to keep you quiet and make you able to stand yourself, if you need to be entertained all the time, there is something wrong with you, not with Jesus. You have not found the pleasure of knowing Him. You have not found what He can be to you. You do not know what He is to you, or else you would not be wasting time.

He is the draw of the Christian, the pleasure of the Christian. Jesus Christ, the Great Shepherd, has power over sin in your life. It is not necessary for Christians to live under the domination and the power of sin. We do not have to do it. Jesus Christ is the Great Shepherd, able to set us free from sin's powers and its domination. Paul said in Romans 7:24&25, " O wretched man that I am! Who shall deliver me from the body of this death? I thank God through Jesus Christ our Lord . . ." So the Lord Jesus Christ saves us from the penalty of sin as the Good Shepherd, and He saves us from the power of sin as the Great Shepherd.

III. THE CHIEF SHEPHERD

The third reference to Jesus' Shepherd-hood, calls Him the Chief Shepherd. It says in the Bible that he is the Chief Shepherd. The Chief Shepherd will save you from the presence of sin. I Peter 5:4- says, "And when the chief Shepherd shall appear, ye shall receive a crown of glory that fadeth not away."

The psalm that presents the Chief Shepherd is Psalm 24. Just as Psalm 22 presents the Good Shepherd and Psalm 23 presents the Great Shepherd, Psalm 24 presents the Chief Shepherd, when He shall come as King of Kings and Lord of Lords.

I can tell you this much about the Holy Land. Sometimes shepherds went out in groups in the Holy Land. They would get out somewhere, and set up a camp, or headquarters. One shepherd would have his flock, another his flock, another his flock, and so on. Each shepherd would go off in his chosen way, but the chief shepherd stayed at the tent, or headquarters.

They took his advice. They did what he said. When they had a sick sheep, they would leave it in his care. He would treat it and doctor it, and bring it back to health. There was a chief shepherd in the group.

The Bible takes that picture, and presents Jesus as the Chief Shepherd. But you know that Christ has some other shepherds. In the Bible, the word "pastor" means shepherd. You have a shepherd. He is an under shepherd to Jesus. He is not the chief one. He is the under shepherd. He is under authority of the Chief Shepherd. The chief shepherd in the Holy Land gave orders to all the other shepherds. They obeyed him. If he said, "You'd better not go over here today to this area", they listened to him. He directed them. They had to obey his authority. You know what? He did not give his orders to the sheep. He gave his orders to the other shepherds the under shepherds. No shepherd ever asked his sheep to vote.

When the shepherd called out his 100 sheep, or however many he had, he called each one of them by name, and they would line up behind him. He did not say, there are a lot of pastures, some have good water but the grass is not so good. Or, there is lot of fine grass but the water is not so good. He did not say, I will let you make up your mind which way you are going to go. The place with lots of good grass has rocks in the water that might mess up your right hind leg. Oh, hogwash. No, he knew where he was going. He just led the way.

The Chief Shepherd gives orders to his own shepherds and they obey Him. As the Chief Shepherd, He cannot save you from the presence of sin yet; that has to wait for Him to come again. For now we are living in the presence of sin all the time. There is sin in the world about you. There is sin in you. Paul said that sin was in his flesh, and he lived in a world of sin and sinners. Sin is present all over the world. You cannot get out of it. You may as well not try.

There were some hermits that tried to hide from it and found out that behind those stone walls in monasteries, sin could still get in . They said that God had betrayed them; they began to hate each other. They became so bitter and depressed that some of them committed suicide. You cannot build a stone wall and hide from sin. It is all about you. There is no way you can get rid of it in this world. You are not going to run it out. It is going to stay here. That is why I am not a reformer. I am not going to waste my time like that.

You cannot eliminate sin. Despite all the people who have worked at it, no noticeable results can be seen. You cannot do it by torture or through education, nor can you do it by philosophy and psychology, as many try to do today, nor can you do it by legislation. You cannot do it by military power. There is no way in the world to eliminate sin from this world. It cannot be done by the elimination of poverty, riches, or sickness. The world systems and world powers that do not recognize sin still believe it exists on its own. They believe it is something man can remove if only he exists without God. They think if we all have free bubbly and adequate rainbow stew, everyone will be peace loving, satisfied, and righteous.

But we know sin is the result of a nature that came from Adam, our father according to the flesh. Romans 3:10 says, " . . . There is none righteous, no not one." I believe that includes you and me. Adam's sons and daughters cannot eliminate that which they produce by natural birth, so they must be born again (Born of God, John 3:6). Only the Chief Shepherd can remove sin from this earth when He comes again.

We can combat it, and must, and we can retard it, but it is still here. It has been here ever since old Satan said he would be like the Most High, and set his throne above the stars of God. So God cast him down to earth (Isaiah 14:12-15) and sin came into this universe. We have to live here with it.

We know, however, that the Great Shepherd has power over the power of sin. We do not have to be beaten by sin. The Great Shepherd can keep us from having to succumb to the powers of sin. But we cannot get it out of the universe. It will be here until He comes, and when He comes, He will save us from the very presence of sin. Hebrews 9:28 says, " . . . unto them that look for him shall he appear the second time without sin unto salvation." That will be a glorious day. It will get sin out of the way - take it out forever and ever. I will surely be glad to see the day that Jesus Christ comes and puts the devil and sin out of business, totally out of business, and as the Chief Shepherd He will accomplish that purpose. He will deliver us from the bondage and the presence of sin when He comes back to this world, and praise God for His coming back! I look forward to that day, when he comes as the Chief Shepherd to gather His sheep. The whole universe will be liberated from the bondage and the power of sin in the presence of God. He will put this creation back in perfect order. Romans, Chapter 8 teaches that.

The Good Shepherd saves us from the penalty of sin, the Great Shepherd from the power of sin, and the Chief Shepherd will deliver us from the presence of sin. That should free us totally from it all. That floors me. I do not know about you, but I will be glad when the Chief Shepherd comes.

We have a Great Shepherd, a wonderful one. I hope you become acquainted with Him through this book. He has never failed me.

The Lord is my Shepherd. Is He yours?

Chapter Two

THE LIFE OF THE SHEPHERD

The Lord is my shepherd; I shall not want. He maketh me to lie down in green pastures; he leadeth me beside the still waters. He restoreth my soul: he leadeth me in the paths of righteousness for his name's sake. (Psalm 23: 1-3)

Verily, verily, I say unto you, He that entereth not by the door into the sheepfold, but climbeth up some other way, the same is a thief and a robber. But he that entereth in by the door is the shepherd of the sheep. To him the porter openeth; and the sheep hear his voice: and he calleth his own sheep by name, and leadeth them out. And when he putteth forth his own sheep, he goeth before them, and the sheep follow him: for they know his voice." (John 10:1-4)

The life of a shepherd in the Holy Land is different from the life of a shepherd anywhere else in the world. In fact, the shepherd's life in the Holy Land is unique in the history of man. It is just peculiar in its nature. The shepherd lived outdoors most of the time with his sheep and underwent the pilgrim life, a hard life with all of its hardships. He lived with his sheep by day and by night. He faced everything out there first. He went before them, and faced every sort of condition that anyone could face as a shepherd in the Holy Land. His was a unique life in many ways. I am ascribing this way of life very directly to the Lord Jesus as our shepherd because that is what

David said: "The Lord is my Shepherd."

Certainly the life of Jesus Christ was a unique one as a shepherd to His people. It stands alone, distinct, and underestimated. There is no other like it. You will not find anything like the life of the Lord Jesus in all the history of man. No one else ever lived the life He did.

We will study the shepherd's life as it <u>was</u> in the Holy Land, (not much there today) showing you how Jesus fulfilled it in His life. Psalm 95:7 says, "For he is our God; and we are the people of his pasture, and the sheep of his hand . . . " Also in Psalm 100:3, " . . . we are his people, and the sheep of his pasture".

I. THE SHEPHERD'S LIFE IS A LOWLY LIFE

The task of being a shepherd was considered a low and menial task. Nobody ever wanted it. It was a hard task, and it was counted as a task for a lesser person, a nobody. It was a very menial thing. This is why in many cases the youngest son was appointed to be a shepherd. The older boys were more important in Jewish families. The family would always make the youngest son take care of the sheep. David was the youngest of eight boys. So he was assigned as the shepherd to take care of the sheep, because that was too lowly a job for the older boys. In Bible times if a man did not have a younger son, sometimes he would make a daughter a shepherdess. Rachel was a shepherdess, daughter of Laban, as we read in Genesis 29:9. Jethro's daughters were shepherdesses until Moses fled there. Then their father, Jethro, made him the shepherd; Moses became a servant of Jethro. That is where Moses, as Exodus, Chapters 2 and 3 record, learned meekness. He was the meekest man who ever lived.

Moses learned as a shepherd of the sheep. Joseph, you recall, was also a shepherd of the sheep, as were his older brothers. The Lord Jesus Christ, though he was The Son of God came from glory, and became such a shepherd. He came into this world and became lowly, humble and meek. In Matthew 11:29, He tells us, "Take my yoke upon you, and learn of me; for I am meek and lowly in heart".

This word "lowly" sometimes means meek, but there is a difference in the two, meek and lowly. Lowly has to do with a position or station in life. Meek has to do with the spirit or attitude of it. There are a lot of people who will get in a lowly position, but they think they do not have a lot of time to stay there. They are resentful, they are proud, and will not be meek long. But Jesus came as the Good Shepherd, and was lowly and meek all the days of His earthly journey. He stooped down to the lowly position. He was born of peasant parents, died on a lowly cross, and was buried in a borrowed tomb. He lived as a nobody in the land where He was born.

He was hated and despised of His own, by His own people. He was in a lowly station, and He was also meek in spirit. The only one that was meeker than Moses was Jesus. Moses was a type of Jesus and Christ fulfilled that type. Moses said, God would provide for the Israelites "a prophet . . . like unto me" (Deuteronomy 18:15). That is what God did. He (JESUS CHRIST) is, that Prophet. Moses stood as the greatest prophet until Jesus.

The Scriptures speak of the humility of Jesus. His whole life was a life of humility. He was misunderstood; He was lowly. He stooped to the level of the lowest of servants. He washed the feet of His disciples as a servant, taking a station of low degree. He always had that spirit of meekness about Him. The lowest station He took was when He went to the cross under your sin and mine. The Lord's position in the eyes of God at that moment was the state of a sinner. He became sin for us. In God's eyes you can be no lower than just to be sin. That is the lowest level. Christ Jesus identified Himself with you and I in that situation. He came and took that position, in the spirit of meekness, and called upon us to follow Him, to have that same meek spirit. There is just no place for pride in the life of a Christian.

I think God hates self-righteous pride more than He does adultery, maybe more than He does murder, because a proud person is the kind of person who will murder. If "Old Lucifer, the angel of the morning, the son of light", be found in you, there is pride. God hates pride and self-righteousness. Those Jesus berated so severely were the Pharisees, because of their pride. Read the woes that Jesus pronounced upon the Pharisees. Talk about rugged - we are talking about tough. Those are tough words.

One might think Jesus was a madman who did not know what He was saying, that He was hating people. But he did not hate them; it was their attitude that He despised. They trusted in themselves, they were self-righteous, proud people. Jesus had more condemnation for pride than anything else. We have to be lowly and meek to be like Him. But too many of us are scrambling for the high places.

We want to be known. We want to be renowned. We want people to look up to us and say, 'Look at him, he is so prayerful." Pharisees make long prayers. "Look at him. Why, he is really a bold Christian. He wears the scriptures all over his clothes. And oh, look at him. He goes to church all the time, and sits on the front row all the time. Our Savior put that all out of business when He came. He stooped from the highest position in the universe to the lowest one possible, became lowly, and was our Good Shepherd. Meek and lowly, He fulfilled that role perfectly as a shepherd of the Holy Land, manifesting the shepherd's life.

II THE SHEPHERD'S LIFE IS A LONELY LIFE

The shepherd of the Holy Land lived a lonely life, very, very lonely. Life for a shepherd in the Holy Land took him away from home for months and months, in places where he seldom saw anybody. If he did see anyone, it was probably a thief or thieves, trying to kill or steal his sheep.

He did not have companionship. His only companionship was his sheep. He lived with his sheep. Occasionally he might see another shepherd. He was alone by day and by night, just with his sheep.

The shepherd would many times sit down somewhere by himself. That is where I think David learned to play that reed flute he made out of cane that grew there. He learned to be a musician as well. He was just a young kid, out there taking care of the sheep.

He would play out there, lonely, to entertain himself. No question about it, shepherds had to live a lonely life. I think Jesus Christ as the Good Shepherd was the loneliest man that ever lived on this earth. Nobody understood Him. Not even His own disciples could understand. He was in a crowd, but you can be alone in a crowd. That might be the loneliest place in the world anyway, with the crowd not caring anything about you, knowing nothing about you. The Bible said that they all forsook Him and fled, left Him alone. Isaiah 63.3 says, "I have trodden the winepress alone; and of the people there was none with me . . . " Peter said, "I will die for you, I will not leave you." Do not jump on Peter, the rest of the crowd also ran off.

Mark wrote in his Gospel, chapter 14, verse 50, "And they all forsook him, and fled." Peter sat down by the devil's fire. Jesus was forsaken of men.

They absolutely left Him by Himself. And not only that, God forsook Him. In Matthew 27:46 Jesus cried, " . . . My God, my God, why hast thou forsaken me?" No one helped Him; no one could. He was left alone.

Did you ever think how long the Son of God was away from His real home? For thirty-three years, He did not get to go to His heavenly home once. Did not get to walk in and look on His Father's face once in thirty-three years – a lonely life. He did it all for us. I believe one of the greatest horrors of hell will be the loneliness of it. I think about Jude 13, which speaks of, " . . . wandering stars, to whom is reserved the blackness of darkness forever." You know what that means? It's speaking of a star cut loose from its orbit, that has no relationship to anything. It is just out there, with no relationship to time, nor place, nor events, nor persons; it is all alone. Jesus tasted every consequence of hell for you and me. He endured it all. The cross was Jesus Christ's loneliest moment. He was all by Himself, with every demon in the world and the devil tormenting Him - all by Himself. The life of a shepherd is a lonely life.

III. THE SHEPHERD'S LIFE IS A LABORIOUS LIFE

Paul writes in I Thessalonians 1:3, "Remembering without ceasing your work of faith, and labor of love, and patience of hope in our Lord Jesus Christ . . ." Being a shepherd requires hard work. It is not something easy; it is tough going. It is tough for many reasons; let me give you three.

First of all, the shepherd lived with his sheep day and night away from his family. He faced the wild beasts. Of course, the beasts in the Holy Land are gone now, for the most part. Back then there was real shepherd life; there were bears, lions, wolves, packs of scavenger dogs, and vipers, and the shepherd also had to be constantly on the watch for thieves. The wild beasts that destroy sheep could kill him as well. This was tough living, a hard life filled with wild beasts, and then wicked thieves.

Thieves would travel three or more in a group, hide somewhere, and watch the shepherd lead a string of sheep, maybe a hundred of them, one behind the other. They would let him almost get by them, jump out, grab the sheep, and steal them. He had to be ever watchful for the thieves. The thieves would jump on him and kill him if possible. That is why he carried his rod, his sling and many other instruments, which I will discuss in chapter 4.

Then he faced severe weather. In that part of that country, there will be huge differences in the temperature between the daytime and the night. There would be hot burning eastern sun by day, then bitter cold at night. The shepherd would lie at night in the door to the sheepfold, and sleep in the cold. The Bible makes mention of the frost that came on Jacob, while he tended the flocks for Laban (Genesis 31:40). He had to face it. It was a laborious life because of the perils there.

Then it was laborious because it was a pilgrim's life. I mean by that, he traveled a lot. He had to climb mountains, go down in valleys, get over big rocks, go from one ledge of rocks to another ledge level. He had to work his way through thorns and thistles, cross streams of water which were sometimes swift enough to sweep him away, always searching for grass and water where his sheep could be nourished. He lived on few rations. He had a little bag and carried some with him, but he didn't have much. He had to be careful. He probably drank a little milk from the sheep, and ate a little cheese he had made. He needed to ration his food. He led a pilgrim's life; that is a hard life. Our pilgrim fathers had a hard time in North America. But we have lost that pilgrim life now. We want things to be easy, to be comfortable. The pilgrim nature of the shepherd's life made it a hard, laborious life.

The shepherd's life of labor had a daily program that he had to follow. First of all, he had to rise early. The shepherd and his sheep in the Holy Land would be up around 3AM, because sheep graze better in the early hours when the dew is on the grass. Later there will sometimes be difficulty in finding water. If the sheep have plenty of dew they will not get as thirsty later in the day.

The water from the grass is better for them. If they do not have cool mornings to graze in, they may go hungry in the heat because they cannot graze well in heat. So the shepherd would rise early to lead his sheep to a place of grass and water. It was a long day. Not just an eight-hour day, a long day. The shepherd did not come in until the sun had set and it was dark, because sheep cannot walk far in the heat; they will become exhausted.

The shepherd would bring the sheep late at night to the sheepfold; then stand in the door, or sometimes he would sit in the door. It was just an opening. Sometimes the shepherd would stand and act as the door. Every sheep that came in went under the rod. If a sheep had a cut place, or thorns, or thistles, or rocks in a foot, or had fever, the shepherd would notice. The shepherd would place the sheep that needed help aside until they were all in the fold. It could be five to ten sheep that had to be treated before he ever put them in, so it could be late in the night by the time he got all of the sheep in.

He had the constant care of the sheep. Day and night the shepherd had to take care of them. Many times he would pick a sheep up, put it on his shoulder and carry it to where he was going next, if it was too weak to go. Often he would take a little lamb that was born on the journey and carry it in his bosom, sometimes more than one at a time. He would help the ones who were about to give birth, the ewes that were heavy with lambs, helping them along. A shepherd had a hard life, a laborious life.

John 21:25 says, "And there are also many other things which Jesus did, the which, if they should be written every one, I suppose that the world itself could not contain the books that should be written." Jesus was a busy man. He never wasted a minute. He said, "I must work the works of him that sent me, while it is day: the night cometh, when no man can work" (John 9:4). No one gave himself to such labor as did Jesus. He was a laboring man. He worked hard as a carpenter, in the carpenter's shop. Then in His ministry for three and a half years, He put in full time and overtime. He did not get much sleep. Working all day long, often praying all night long. He would stay out to talk to His father and pray, and the next morning, without sleep, go back to the multitude, and bear their burdens. He was a hard worker. The shepherd's life is a laborious life.

IV. THE SHEPHERD'S LIFE IS A LOVING LIFE

I tell everybody that the Good Shepherd gave His life for the sheep (John 10:11). "Greater love hath no man than this, that a man lay down his life for his friends" (John 15:13). He loved them; that is why He died for them. The relation of a shepherd to sheep in the Holy Land was not just the relationship of a man to an animal. There was more to it than that. There was a friendship and fellowship between the shepherd and the sheep, a very close one. He loved the sheep and the sheep loved him. The shepherd loved his sheep enough to die for them. The shepherd had a special love for each of his sheep. In the morning, whenever the shepherd would take the sheep from the fold, he would get in front and call them by name. Each one had a place in their grazing line or file line. When it was called, it would take its place in line.

If the shepherd had a hundred, each had its place. They would line up, a hundred in line and start off to the grass. The shepherd let them feed on the grass in the early morning, so they could get both the dew and the grass. Sometimes during the day, he would stop, and turn around and look at his sheep. Down that line a sheep would step out of line and look up at the shepherd, coming toward him with a soft "baa, baa." The shepherd would stick out his hand, the sheep would come, and he would take that sheep, rub it on the head, rub its ears, scratch it on the chin, pat it on its shoulder, stroke its back and pick it up and fondle it. That is how you show love for an animal: fondle it. Then he might put the sheep on his shoulder. He loved them.

Whenever a sheep would come to him, he would stoop down and lift an ear up, and talk to that sheep. Ask it how the grass was, did it have a good day, did it think the shepherd had been good to it that day; actually talk in the ear of the sheep. Given that expression of love, the sheep would go back to its place, and get in line. Others would come out the same way. He loved them. He fondled them. The shepherd loved his sheep enough to die for them. He would fight the enemies, regardless of how many were there. They were his sheep, and he would kill all their enemies he could. He loved his sheep. The shepherd had a special, peculiar love for his sheep that he had for nobody else, or anything else in this world. Jesus loves His sheep. He is the Great Good Shepherd. He loves them.

There is two-fold evidence that He does. First, there are the many provisions He has made. The shepherd out of love provided everything essential for the sheep, everything. The Bible said that God gave Christ for us and shall also freely give us all things (Romans 8:32). By His provisions He evidenced His love for the sheep. If you do not love them, you will not provide for them. A hireling will not provide for the sheep. A hireling will run off and leave them, let them starve, even let the beasts kill them, but a shepherd will give his life for the sheep.

God loved us enough to provide everything necessary. Jesus Christ, our

Good Shepherd, showed how much He loved us by His sacrificial death. The price He paid for you and I on the cross confirmed His love. Paul said that Jesus" . . . loved me and gave Himself for me" (Galatians 2:20), - not just the world, but me. So having loved us, He died for us. He gave Himself in total sacrifice on the cross out of that love. The shepherd's life was certainly a loving life.

V. THE SHEPHERD'S LIFE IS A LIFTING LIFE

Psalms 40:1-3 indicates this. "I waited patiently for the Lord; and he inclined unto me, and heard my cry. He brought me up also out of an horrible pit, out of the miry clay, and set my feet upon a rock, and established my goings. And he hath put a new song in my mouth, even praise unto our God: many shall see it, and fear, and shall trust in the Lord".

The shepherds actually did a lot of lifting physically. They would pick wounded sheep up and lay them around their neck on their shoulders. The shepherd would lift the new lambs up and carry them in his bosom. He would take the weak ewes, who had grown faint before the birth of a lamb and carry them. He actually lifted them a lot of the time, especially in the valley of the shadow of death in the Holy Land. That valley is just twelve feet wide in the widest place, and sometimes, walking downhill, they first had to get up to a higher level to get out. The shepherd would take his staff, sometimes put the crook under the front legs of a lamb, and lift it up on the level where he was. If it were a grown sheep, he would put the crook around its neck and lift it up to his level. He always had to be lifting them up. The shepherd always brought the sheep up, and the Lord Jesus Christ lifts us. That is what this Psalm is about. "He lifted me up out an horrible pit, out of the miry clay."

The fact is that the shepherd lived for the betterment and the uplifting of the sheep. He wanted to always improve their lives. He wanted to make them better. He wanted to make them fat, let them produce wool, and to enrich them in every way. Christ, our faithful and Great Shepherd, lived that kind of life. All he wants is to lift you up, to bless you, to elevate you spiritually.

He lifts us out of. Notice, "he brought me up also out of the horrible pit, out of the miry clay". He lifts us out of. He lifts us out of the penalty of sin.

The pit means death for you, for sin brings the death penalty. When Christ saves you he lifts you out of that pigpen. The penalty for sin is death.

Then he lifts you out of the power of sin. Notice it says, "lifts me up out of that horrible pit, out of the miry clay". You are no more under the control of the miry clay. He lifts you out of the power of sin.

I want to make this clear. Jesus does not save people in their sin. He saves them <u>out of</u> their sin. Out of the guilt of it, out of the penalty of it, out of the power of it.

Sin not only has a penalty and power, but it pollutes you. It makes you filthy, and the pit you enter is like a deep well, with perpendicular walls. The rainwater would run down, and wash dirt and debris on the one in the pit. Sometimes you get so filthy and dirty you cannot stand yourself, an immoral uncleanness. Jesus Christ cleanses us from that immorality of life. Jesus cleanses the filth of life away. You do not love that life anymore. Sin is a filthy thing, it pollutes you, makes you unclean, and God will not have companionship or communion with us until we are lifted out of it. The Good Great Chief Shepherd lifts us out of the penalty of sin, the power of sin, and the pollution of sin.

Not only does the shepherd lift out, he also lifts upon. "He sat my feet upon a rock." I want to define that rock for you. First of all, The Great Shepherd sets you upon the rock of His presence. Upon this rock, Himself, "I will build my church" (Matthew 16:17). You are on the foundation of Jesus Christ; you are built on Him. That is a very stable foundation. If the foundation were Peter, it fell before it started, because Peter cursed the Savior and denied His God-ordained destiny. (Matthew 16:22&23) Peter died later in life, after Pentecost. So the church was not to be built on Peter.

We are put upon the ROCK OF JESUS CHRIST (Matthew 7.24). Not only does He lift us out of, and upon, but He lifts us into. He lifts us first of all into a path, "for he established my goings". He sent me away from the pit. He got me marching away in the other direction from where I had been. It is a progressive thing, going farther and farther from sin, more and more toward the Lord. That is what this scripture teaches us.

Then He lifted me into plenty of provision. Psalm 23 reads, "I shall not want." God, through Christ Jesus has plenty of provision for you and me. If we are living a pauper's life, it is because we are not appropriating the provision that has been provided for us.

Then He lifts us into the praise of proclamation. Psalm 40:3 reads, "And he hath put a new song in my mouth, even praise unto our God . . ." This whole psalm shows the lifting out, lifting into and the gratefulness, for He put a new song in my heart.

Look at the content of this proclamation. It is praise. "A new song in my heart." That is the new song of redemption, of deliverance, that is because we are a new creation, we have not been here before. We were lost but now are found, we were dead in sin, but are now quickened by His spirit and made alive.

When you get redeemed, you have a song of redemption. That is the content of this proclamation of praise He lifted you into. I want you to understand the object of this praise. This is very important. The object of the proclamation is praise unto our God. We are not to praise deliverance, or the experience of salvation we have had. We are to praise the Deliverer. I do not take much stock in testimonial meetings we have. We import some old football player from somewhere, that kicked a football on Sunday, bring him in, put him up in these big evangelical crusades to tell how he got saved. He talks about how much he was in sin, how much he did, and what part he played in getting saved, all that talk about his experience, around and around he spins, never says anything about Jesus. That is all backward.

It seems when we have a praise service, the first thing you hear folks praising is themselves. If you have been lifted up by the Shepherd, you are out of the horrible pit, and you should praise Him for doing that. Praise unto our God, the Redeemer. There are songs written about human experience. Songwriters are not writing songs of praise any more, but songs about themselves, about what happened inside their experience, their internal change, but without any praise unto God. The Lord, our Good Shepherd, saved and lifted us out like a shepherd. Praise Him! We do not praise the redeeming; we praise the Redeemer.

An old songwriter a long time ago wrote (and I love this song) He Lifted Me. "In loving kindness, Jesus came, my soul in mercy to reclaim. And from the depths of sin and shame, through grace He lifted me.

"From sinking sand, He lifted me. With tender hands, He lifted me. From shades of night to planes of light, all praise His name. He lifted me."

You have to get your praise right. It is right to praise Him.

Chapter Three

THE SPIRIT OF THE SHEPHERD

"He Restoreth My Soul"

The spirit is everything with God. Sins from attitudes and sins of the spirit are the worst sins in God's sight. Not the sins of external acts, or of the flesh, but sins of the spirit, and sins of the heart.

Take the matter of pride, pride of spirit. God hates pride as no sin you will find in the Bible, so the spirit is of great importance to God. I have seen people who were externally right do some mighty good external deeds and then ruin them with a nasty spirit. So spirit is vastly important.

A man's spirit is the most important thing about him in determining everything else about him - his words, his acts, his motives, and all of his life. The shepherd in the Holy Land had his spirit marked with certain unique traits or characteristics. Concerning our Shepherd, Isaiah records for us in Chapter 11, verse 2: "And the spirit of the Lord shall rest upon him, the spirit of wisdom and understanding, the spirit of counsel and might, the spirit of knowledge and of the fear of the Lord." Paul writes in Philippians 2:3, "Let nothing be done through strife or vainglory; but in lowliness of mind let each esteem other better than themselves."

I. THE SHEPHERD HAS A SPIRIT OF AFFECTION (LOVE)

That is what Isaiah is writing about. " . . . he shall gather the lambs with his arm, and carry them in his bosom, and shall gently lead those that are with young" (Isaiah 40:11). Also in John 10:15 (Jesus speaking), " . . . I lay down my life for the sheep." No shepherd would ever qualify in the Holy Land to take care of a flock of sheep if he did not love them. He would be disqualified. He would be accounted as a hireling that did not care a thing about the sheep. The only thing that he was out for was the money, what he could get, or the pay he could receive. You could not be a shepherd if you did not love the sheep.

To be a shepherd and see after the sheep, you had to love them. That is true of the Good Shepherd, the Great Shepherd, and the Chief Shepherd, the Lord Jesus Christ. He loves His sheep. He loved them enough to die for them. His sheep are God's people, of course. We are His sheep, the sheep of His pasture; we are the people of God, and He loves us. That affection and love are traits that a shepherd must have.

In the first place, His love was marked by compassion. The Scripture says Jesus looked upon the multitudes and saw them as sheep scattered without a shepherd, and He was moved with compassion (Matthew 9:36). "Moved" is a strong word. It really means He convulsed. Have you ever cried until you felt that if you cried one more time your whole insides would come out? Have you ever been hurt so deeply that you were pained on the inside? Or have you ever gotten so tickled you thought if you laughed one more giggle that would be the end of you? Well, that is mild compared to what Jesus thought, when He looked upon the multitude without a shepherd. Scattered like sheep, He was moved with compassion. The word "compassion" is used 16 times in the four Gospels, concerning Jesus. How He was moved with compassion.

The Bible says that His bowels were moved with compassion, and that means all the inner parts of Jesus. That means His heart, His liver, all the rest inside Him was suffering pain when He looked upon the people. He was moved with compassion. That is because he loved them. That is affection. Then affection must be marked with the trace of pity. This matter of being pious and sympathizing is not affection. Pity means more than sympathy. It means empathy - to feel with them. James said in James 5:11, ". . . the Lord is very pitiful, and of tender mercy." Jesus felt what the people felt. He shared in their suffering. It was in tune with His heart of affection.

A shepherd always had his affection marked with tenderness. The scripture says that he would lead them gently (Isaiah 40:11). A shepherd could not deal cruelly, or harshly and roughly with the sheep at all. He would not get anywhere with them. They could not take it. They would flee from him if he was harsh or rough, or if his voice was cruel and abrasive. There had to be tenderness in the voice of the shepherd, full of pathos and kindness. In dealing with the sheep, the shepherd had to be filled with tenderness. Then a shepherd's affection had to be marked by gentleness. A shepherd could not just walk in an audacious way and start dealing roughly with his sheep. He had to be gentle. A sheep will not respond to anything but gentleness, not roughness or boisterousness.

That affection was marked by patience. You just think sheep will never arrive. They can get into more jams, more messes, cause you more heartache, more trouble than most any animal, because they are so defenseless, they are so helpless, they are in such danger all the time. Revelation 1:9 speaks of the patience of Jesus Christ. Did you ever think about how patient Jesus had to be? Over and over and over He would ask them, "Oh ye of little faith, why do you not believe? How long must I bear with you?" Were it not for the patience of our Shepherd, we would already be in hell.

There is not one of us that deserves His patience. He puts up with lot of bickering. He bears our troubles. I do not mean that He just merely endures it. He is patient in it. You know what patience is? It's faithfulness under pressure. Jesus' own faith was under the deepest pressure. It did not matter where trials came from; He was patient. Affection was marked with kindness. The word kind comes from kin: k-i-n. You are supposed to be kind to your kin. Jesus identified Himself with the sheep, so He was like kinfolks to them, and He had kindness toward them. He was never cruel or harsh. He never dealt with His disciples in harsh terms. He always dealt with them in truth, but He was kind in it. His kindness was always in evidence when dealing with the people.

I have heard some professing Christians say, "I will tell them off." That is not any credit to them. That is not like Jesus. They are not following in His steps. "I'll put him in his place." That is not like our Shepherd, not like the Savior. That is not the way His Spirit works. He has kindness for His people, His sheep. I am reminded of the scripture in Lamentations 3:21-23, "This I recall to my mind, therefore have I hope. It is of the Lord's mercies that we are not consumed, because his compassions fail not. They are new every morning: great is thy faithfulness."

One more thing that marked the affection of the shepherd - he was longsuffering. Not only does it mean just to bear, but it means to suffer with. He suffered with them. The shepherd when he started to bring a flock along would spend long hours, long days, and long months. He had to take the little lambs and bear with them and suffer over them and keep on nurturing and nurturing in order to bring them to maturity. The Lord Jesus Christ in His affection had to do that with every one of us, and still does. He has to be longsuffering. In fact, I think He does it over our whole lifetime; He continues longsuffering. These are some of the essential elements in this spirit of affection that a shepherd must have, if he is to be a good shepherd to the sheep. Certainly all these traits mark the love of the Lord Jesus Christ for His people who are called the sheep of God's pasture. Peter wrote in II Peter 3:15, "And account that the longsuffering of our Lord is salvation . . ."

II. THE SHEPHERD HAS A SPIRIT OF SOLICITATION

The Word of God says that Jesus came into this world " . . . to seek and to save that which was lost" (Luke 19:10). Solicitation means to seek after. He was always solicitous. The shepherd in the Holy Land cared for the welfare of the sheep. Everything he did was solicitous for the betterment of the sheep. Constantly he worked on their behalf. He was ever thoughtful of their needs. He was constantly providing every provision. They could not provide for themselves; the shepherd had to provide for them. He was solicitous for their welfare continually.

Jesus said in John 10:16, "And other sheep I have which are not of this fold: them also I must bring . . . " Again, He was seeking after their welfare. That is what happened when one went astray. The shepherd went after it, sought it, found it, brought it on his shoulder, and returned with it to the fold, to the flock, rejoicing over the fact he had found it. The sheep are never solicitous about the shepherd, but the shepherd is very solicitous about the sheep. Sheep do not have much sense about why to mind the shepherd. They do not seek him much. They are pretty weak in their efforts to seek the shepherd, but not the shepherd the sheep. He is the one that takes the initiative to go after them, find them, and recover them, because he is solicitous. He has their welfare at heart, and he bears them all the time in his heart.

The shepherd must have the spirit of solicitation. If you do not care about the sheep, you will never make a shepherd. If you are not really willing to be solicitous about them, you will certainly not take care of them. That is what brought Jesus Christ down here to find you and me. He was solicitous about us, as lost sheep, so He came to seek and save that which was lost. The Son of Man came to seek and save that which was lost. In the 15th Chapter of Luke, it says that the shepherd had one lost sheep, and he went after it and sought it until he found it. That is Jesus, The Great and Good Shepherd seeking after us.

A shepherd must have a spirit of solicitation. This spirit should also be a mark of the sheep of his pasture. We should also be solicitous about the welfare of others. We should be concerned about the welfare of each another. In the church, family, or business today it seems we have lost the spirit of our Shepherd. We say it does not matter. Just let them get along as best they can; it is none of our business. We did not have anything to do with their problems. Every day you hear of this attitude in the church. You are breaking fellowship, and you are scattering the sheep. We should be solicitous like the shepherd toward each another, about the welfare of one another.

III. THE SHEPHERD HAS A SPIRIT OF INTERVENTION

I mean by that, courage. A shepherd had to be courageous in the Holy Land. There are all kinds of dangers that sheep face. The shepherd had to courageously face the enemies of the sheep, and the enemies were wild ferocious animals. The lions, the bears, the leopards, and then packs of wolves, and not only that but packs of scavenger dogs, big dogs that would tear them all to pieces, and eat the meat off. He had to face all these dangers, and not be a coward that would leave the sheep. That is what a hireling would do. He would see a wolf coming and leave the sheep because he is a coward. He would be afraid to face it.

The shepherd in the Holy Land had to face the storms. In those desert lands, storms would come, the wind could blow sheep over, scatter them everywhere, and the animals would destroy them. But the shepherd would not leave them. He faced the storm. He would look for some great rock to lead them to, and he would not rest until they all were under the shadow of that great rock to protect them. He would face the storm instead. The shepherd was courageous also in that he faced the thieves and the robbers. They hid everywhere in the pastures of the Holy Land, watching as the shepherd and sheep came, in order to take them by surprise.

The shepherd many times would face three or four thieves alone. He had to be courageous. You know about our Savior don't you? There were not any enemies that scared Him off. Even when the devil, fierce circumstances of life, and terrible mockery were arrayed against Him, trying to destroy His good name, everything, He stood courageous in His determination. He faced the cross bravely. You know why? He was concerned about the sheep. He was not concerned about Himself. He was concerned about His people - the sheep of His pasture.

He was courageous. Nothing could turn Him aside. Nothing could cause Him to fear. He went forth in faith to face the enemies of the souls of men. Our Good Shepherd had such courage that when they came with Judas to take Him to be crucified, they asked if He was Jesus of Nazareth and He simply said, "I am He," and went with them.

IV. THE SHEPHERD HAS A SPIRIT OF CONSIDERATION

Thoughtfulness and care preoccupied the shepherd. He had to be ever mindful of his sheep, day or night. Sometimes a shepherd would grow weary, and maybe get sleepy, but he did not sleep much. He was considering the sheep's welfare. He would put that staff, the crook under his chin sometimes and nap. The least little movement that was not in order brought him up, wide awake. He did everything because of his thoughtfulness for the sheep. Not one time was he ever thoughtless of them. Every morning he knew he had to go somewhere to find grass. You know what he would do? The shepherd would lie awake at night, planning the next day's travels. He was thoughtful of his sheep, considerate of them, always mindful of their needs. In his consideration and thoughtfulness, he was proud for them. He provided in that thoughtfulness, consideration, and care, everything they needed.

Sheep have needs, desperate needs for certain things they cannot do without. They cannot do without grass, they cannot do without water, and they cannot do without protection. They have to have it. There is no way for them to live on their own in the Holy Land. They must have direction and guidance. They need restoration to health when they get sickly, so the shepherd's every thought is about their needs. That is why David said, "I shall not want." The Great Good Shepherd, the Lord Jesus, is considerate of our needs and welfare continually. Peter instructed pastors (or shepherds) to be like-minded in I Peter 5:2-4, "Feed the flock of God which is among you, taking the oversight thereof, not by constraint, but willingly; not for filthy lucre, but of a ready mind; Neither as being lords over God's heritage, but being ensamples to the flock. And when the Chief Shepherd shall appear, ye shall receive a crown of glory that fadeth not away."

V. THE SHEPHERD HAS A SPIRIT OF JUBILATION (JOY)

The one thing the shepherd rejoiced over, more than anything else in his whole life, was his sheep. When they were doing well, he rejoiced over them. He liked to take people out and show them, when they were in good shape, fat and fluffy. He lived to revel in their betterment. Whenever one went astray, it was found and brought back. The shepherd came with it on his shoulder, rejoicing. He had a spirit of jubilation. David would express his jubilation with the reed flute he had made. He would actually play music to the sheep because it had a great effect on them. The fact is, certain types of music were a very definite help to the sheep. Sometimes music would quiet and quell them, make them responsive to the shepherd, and make them move like he wanted them to. Other times he could speed the music up, to make them move faster. The shepherd was jubilant. He did not go around defeated, depressed, grouchy and growling. The sheep picked up his spirit. He was jubilant over them. He sang to them, about them, and he liked to show them off. A shepherd had that kind of spirit. When a shepherd found a lost sheep, he called his friends and neighbors, saying unto them, rejoice with me. (Luke 15:6).

VI. THE SHEPHERD HAS A SPIRIT OF OBSERVATION, ATTENTION AND WATCHFULNESS

There is not one moment, day or night, when the shepherd did not watch over his sheep.

He did not leave them unobserved nor unattended for a moment. He was constantly observing the sheep, watchful. The Bible says that the Lord neither slumbers nor sleeps (Psalm 121:4). He does not go to sleep, and neither does he take a nap. All the while, His eyes are on you, watching over you. If the Great, Good Shepherd of ours did not constantly watch over us, the wicked forces in this world would defeat us. He is constantly watching over us.

That is how the Shepherd is. He is observant of all our needs. He watches over our welfare. He must be one that has the spirit of watchfulness. No shepherd ever walks into a shady nook to lie down, leaving the sheep unobserved. A shepherd did not go somewhere to get a drink of water, and leave the sheep in the dirt. The shepherd would not put them in the fold at night without observing them. When he brought them to the door to let them in, he would pull them in one by one. The shepherd never drove a flock in altogether. A shepherd did not drive his sheep; he led them. He would take his rod and have each sheep pass under it for inspection. The shepherd will drop his rod down so a sheep will have to stop, and he will look at it to see if it is sickly. If so, he takes that rod and pushes it aside to let the next one come. Sometimes he would have eight or ten to tend to. He would doctor some, pull thorns out, maybe put ointment on a sore, or maybe a bite of some kind. He was just always watching after them.

A shepherd did not sleep well at night. He would lie down, and at the least disturbance
among those sheep in the fold, he would be wide awake. If somebody crawled over that wall, if a thief or robber tried to climb up some other way to steal sheep, he would hear them. All day and night he watched over them. If you did not have that sort of protective spirit, you could never be a shepherd. Not back in the Holy Land - not in the day of real shepherds and the sheep life that marked the Holy Land as depicted in the Bible.

There is a spirit of attention and observation, watchfulness, sleeplessness constantly watching over you. You know God never shuts His eyes. He sees you all the time. He is watching you all the time. He knows before the enemy is on his way. He knows before the danger ever meets you in the path. He is already on the way. He is watching it all. I mean with a watchfulness prepared to do something, to help you in your time of need.

VII. THE SHEPHERD HAD A SPIRIT OF PACIFICATION

The psalmist David had such a spirit of tranquility. It was mollifying to the sheep and it would pacify them. If a shepherd got excited and lost his calm, got distressed, fretful and stressed, the sheep would not trust him. He was one that was calm in the midst of all kinds of storms, all kind of pressures. He had a spirit of tranquility and peace in him. Did you ever follow the life of Jesus and see how much harassment He had, and how He calmly went through it? How He peaceably went on. How He went on undisturbed in His tranquility, or how He could go down to the ship, and sleep while the storms were blowing. He could - that is what He did. It did not upset Him. Jesus could turn around and say, "Peace, be still." The waves became passive and the wind stopped. You just could not lead sheep and be one of those excited people, always distressed, always up in the air with no peace, because you would destroy their peace. They would not have any peace around you. So shepherds must have a spirit of tranquility, peace and calm, and they did have. Our Lord and Savior Jesus Christ certainly did.

VIII. THE SHEPHERD HAD A SPIRIT OF DEDICATION AND DEVOTION

He had to be devoted to them and dedicated to them, even to the point of his suffering extreme distress. All he ever did was for them. He lived with them day and night, cared for them, and was constantly serving them. He was never one moment idle, continually exercising devotion and dedication to the whole flock.

IX. THE SHEPHERD HAD A SPIRIT OF SELF-ABNEGATION

When Jesus said, "The Good Shepherd gives His life for the sheep", that is exactly what He meant. The Bible says the Lord Jesus Christ made Himself of no reputation (Philippians 2:7). He was continually denying self for the welfare of the sheep, even to the point of going to the cross and giving His life, for He said in John 10:17&18, " . . . I lay down my life, that I might take it again. No man taketh it from me, but I lay it down of myself . . ." He did it for His sheep. This is the spirit of self-denial.

Did you know shepherds in the Holy Land would do that for their sheep - live apart and deny themselves the comforts of their homes, the conveniences, the better things? They chose to live in the hot sun that could cause sunstroke and fever, face everything, and just deny themselves, so the sheep might be cared for. Self-denial, self-abnegation, that is the Lord Jesus. He never thought of anything for Himself. He came down from His Father's House, and everything He did, He did for the welfare of others, denying Himself the conveniences and the comforts of life. He absolutely denied self and gave Himself in total sacrifice for His sheep. That is the spirit of the shepherd. It is essential in a shepherd in the Holy Land, and it certainly was present in the life of the Lord Jesus Christ. Jesus, the Good Shepherd, had our welfare in mind as He worked the great work of a shepherd on the cross, that He might make it possible for us to become members of His flock and the fold of the people of God.

Chapter Four

THE SHEPHERD'S INSTRUMENTS

"Thy Rod and Thy Staff"

The Lord is my shepherd, I shall not want. He maketh me to lie down in green pastures. He leadeth me beside the still waters. He restoreth my soul. He leadeth me in the paths of righteousness for his name's sake. Yea, though I walk through the valley of the shadow of death, I will fear no evil for thou art with me; thy rod and thy staff they comfort me." (Psalm 23:1-4)

Notice the statement, "thy rod and thy staff they comfort me." This chapter is about the shepherd's instruments - his supplies, or it might be better to say, his equipment.

I have considered the shepherd so far as to his shepherd-hood, his life and his spirit. Now I want to give consideration to the shepherd's instruments. There are certain kinds of instruments, equipment and supplies that the shepherd carried with him at all times, both for his welfare, and for the welfare of the sheep.

Throughout the Bible reference is made to them. These instruments or these supplies the shepherd always carried with him. In this chapter I will not take up all those instruments that are scattered throughout the Bible. I will concentrate on the tools that are mentioned in the Psalm 23, the rod and the staff. The shepherd always had these tools. He could not do without them, if he was to shepherd the sheep. A shepherd always had the rod and the staff to deal with sheep.

I. THE ROD

"Thy rod comforts me," David said. Maybe we should look hard at the nature of the rod. We need to know what it is like so that we understand its use. The rod was a shepherd's club. It was chosen when a young man started to become a shepherd. He would go into the woods and find a sapling, dig it up by the roots, carefully choosing the right kind, one that felt right in his hand. He would cut the roots off, and leave a knot on the end about the size of your fist or a little larger. Then he spent days trimming it, making it just exactly right in weight and length for him. Sometimes rods would be made longer, sometimes heavier than others. It depended on what worked best for the individual shepherd.

He would take that rod, after he trimmed the knob on one end, and drive nails or metal into it. This made it heavier, a more deadly weapon in his hands. A long time before he went into the dangerous areas, he would practice throwing that rod so he could be accurate in striking anything he wanted to hit. He would practice at close range until he was familiar with it, and knew all about it. Thus, one way in which he practiced to become a shepherd was to learn how to use a rod. That describes how the rod was actually used by a shepherd in the land of Palestine. He made it a very deadly weapon in his hands against all kinds of enemies.

The second thing to note is the usage of the rod. What use did the shepherd put it to? In the first place, it was an instrument of warfare - an instrument of protection for himself as the protector of the sheep. He could beat down an animal with it. He could use it against lions, bears, tigers, wolves, or any thief who attacked him or the sheep. It was a vital thing in the Holy Land of days gone by. They did not have guns like we do, but they used the rod with that knob very effectively to fight off enemies, to win any battle against thieves.

The rod also was used for another purpose. It was an instrument of clearance. Many times leading sheep to where he wanted them to go, the shepherd would clear through briers, thorns, thistles, and other kinds of difficult places. You cannot lead sheep a long way. They grow weary and may get sunstroke. So the shepherd would take his rod and go into the thistles and the thorns and beat out a pathway through them while his sheep stood and waited. He would knock down the briers, tear down the cactus and beat down anything that would obstruct their pathway across that particular place. It was an instrument of clearance. The shepherd cleared a pathway for the sheep with his rod.

It was also an instrument of discipline or chastisement for his sheep. Proverbs 29:15 says, "The rod and reproof give wisdom . . . " It is for the sheep's advantage to teach, to discipline, to instruct. Sometimes a sheep would be so unruly that if nothing would correct it, the shepherd would take the rod and might break the sheep's leg, then immediately bind it up, put it on his shoulder, and carry it around with him on his shoulder. When it had mended, that sheep sometimes became the leader of the file line. It was the first one, right up against the shepherd, never to go astray again. They did not go astray after they had a leg broken by the shepherd.

So the rod was for discipline. The Bible talks about you taking the rod, and disciplining your children with the rod, and if you did not use it on them, it says you hate them and do not love them (Proverbs 13:24). The shepherd loved his sheep; therefore he would not allow them to go astray. He would use the rod to correct them and to instruct them.

The rod was also used to number and examine the sheep. I have mentioned before that when the shepherd arrived at the fold at night the sheep all had to pass under the rod. He would take the rod and stop every sheep and thoroughly examine it. If he found something wrong with that sheep, he would make it stand aside. You know what else he would do with the rod? In the Holy Land, there was a disease called the scab. It would get on the body. The sheep would begin doing poorly, lose their wool, and the shepherd could discern this. A shepherd would take his rod and part the wool so he could see with his keen eye the scab and treat it. The statement, you cannot pull the wool over his eyes came from this practice. You could not pull the wool over the shepherd's eyes. He examined you.

David knew this and he used it. In Psalm 139:23-24 he wrote, "Search me, O God, and know my heart: try me, and know my thoughts: and see if there be any wicked way in me, and lead me in the way everlasting." His implied meaning is, "Oh, Shepherd, take your rod and divide the wool and find the scab. Look me totally over." That is what a shepherd would do. Take that rod, just part the wool and completely examine the sheep to find all that was wrong with it, give it a thorough examination. So the rod was used for that purpose also.

We should not shrink from this. We should desire for God to examine us, find our ailments, our wrongs, so we can correct them. We should not run away from Him, walk off from Him, not allowing Him to discipline us, to examine us. We ought to cry out to God to examine us. Whenever you have reached a point of confessing all the sins you know to Him, you are not through. Just stay in the presence of God and ask Him to examine you and test you, because you will not know about all your sins. You will not be honest about all of them. You have secret sins, like the scab under the wool, that maybe you are not conscious of. You should ask God to search you out.

So the shepherd used a rod to number the sheep and examine them. That is how he found out if one was missing when he put them in the fold. He would count them in with the rod and if it was not the right number, he knew he had to go back over the journey to find the one that went astray. The rod was used as an instrument of numbering, and examination, searching out the sheep for its welfare, and its health.

The rod also is a symbol. This word rod means a scepter to rule. It symbolizes authority and power. Hebrews 1:8 says, "But unto the Son he saith, Thy throne, O God, is for ever and ever: a scepter of righteousness is the scepter of thy kingdom." This means He will rule in righteousness, and exercise authority in righteousness. So the rod stands for that, in a particular way. It means the authority and power of the Word of God. Go back to Moses' time; the first time a rod is mentioned in the Bible in an important way is with Moses. You find out that Moses' rod stood for what God said. It represented His authority. The rod represented the Word of God.

God uses His rod, His Word, to protect us against our enemy. God uses it to clear a pathway for our life, and God uses it to examine us and search our hearts.

Was not that what Jesus did? He used the Word against that roaring lion, the devil. He took it as an extra warhead against him and beat him with it. He had victory over him with it. By the way, when Jesus was led into the desert to be tempted by the devil, all the scriptures He used came from one book of the Bible, the book of Deuteronomy. He did not quote from any other book at this time. He took the fifth book of the Bible, which summarizes all the four preceding books of Moses. Jesus won His victory over the devil with that single book. It was like the rod in the hand of the shepherd beating down the enemy, that roaring lion, the devil (Deuteronomy 8:3, Deuteronomy 6:13-16, Matthew 4:1-11).

It is the Word of God that you have to use against him, always remember that. You have an authority and a power in the Word of God against your enemies, if you let the Shepherd make it effective in your life.

I remember reading about David, the shepherd boy with his sling. He took his sling, went down to the brook, and took five smooth stones. They all had to be smooth and round. If you put them in a sling they were not to be rough or flat. The wind would not affect a perfect stone; it would go to its mark.

David used the Word of God to beat Goliath, just as Jesus used it to defeat the devil. Jesus used the fifth book, and David took five stones, but he only needed one. This was what God had said. This is what he is saying to us. The Word of God is the authority and power in the hand of the shepherd to protect the life of the sheep.

The Word of God, your Bible, is the greatest source of comfort in this life. When you find your spirit troubled, harassed and down, you have to get anchored again, established again, the pathway cleared, the fences torn out of the way, so you can walk in the light of God's Word. That is God-given authority and power, the Word of God. That is the rock. You do not have any other; it is all you need.

In Jude 9, he relates that Michael the archangel, when contending with the devil, said " . . .The Lord rebuke you." Jesus, the Good Shepherd used the Word all the time. He used the Word of God against His enemies and also to care for His sheep – instructing them, disciplining them, and searching them out. Oh, how His words searched them out when He spoke. The word of God is the rod and it comforts.

II. THE STAFF

The staff also was a sapling but a longer one, pretty long. A young man becoming a shepherd would need a staff also. He did not dig it up by the root. He would cut if off and trim it, while it was green and pliable. He had a way of bending a crook or a hook on the end and making it permanent. When the shepherd fixed it that way it became a staff. It is very questionable if any other instrument in the Bible so represents the shepherd as the staff. Whenever you see a shepherd, his staff is always nearby. It is the most representative instrument that he had. It stands for him, represents him in a great way.

So the shepherd-to-be would get his staff fixed, let it season until the crook would not unbend nor lose its form and shape when he put it to use. It was another sapling, cut out of the woods, seasoned, made right and fixed to fit the hand of a particular shepherd so he could use it effectively.

The uses of the staff are numerous. These are wonderful things. It blesses my heart to know this. First of all, the shepherd uses the staff to draw sheep together in close intimate relationships. Sheep can get scattered easily. So the shepherd just reaches with the crook of his staff and pulls them back. Many times an old ewe will get all concerned about grazing and forget her lamb. If you let the lamb stay away from her for a long time, she may just completely ignore it the rest of its life.

The shepherd takes the staff and tenderly draws that lamb to the ewe. It is used to draw them into intimate relationship, first of all, to each other. He binds them together to each other. If you want to get a beautiful name for this, in Zechariah it's called Bands (Zechariah 11:7). This staff unites them. The shepherd would keep them together with his staff. Many times in a flock of sheep, timid sheep will not get close to the shepherd, sort of bypass him and go around, yet he will take that staff and reach out and draw that sheep to him, love it, nurture it, and make it more responsive to him.

The staff is used for the purpose of drawing the sheep into an intimate relationship with each other and with the shepherd. That is why it so much represents who he is.

It is used for another purpose. That is to guide the sheep. Many times sheep walk on a dangerous ledge in the Holy Land, especially going into and through the valley of the shadow of the death. The shepherd would often place the staff beside the sheep as they walked through a dangerous place until they were safely across, guiding them, directing them. Giving them the direction they should have. The shepherd used it very effectively to guide the sheep.

More than that, he used his staff to free the sheep from entanglement. Quite often sheep would go astray after grass. Before you knew it, they had walked under some cactus bush, their long wool was entangled and they could not get out. The shepherd with his staff would reach under there and deliver them, free them from the entanglement. These are the three principal uses of the staff of the shepherd: to draw the sheep together, to guide them, and to deliver them from entanglements in their journey through the Holy Land, as they sought grass and water.

I want to tell you what the staff symbolizes. The staff is first of all, a symbol of support, or a stay. It supports the sheep. It was a stay when the sheep were on a journey to pasture. That staff was put against them to stabilize them; it was a support for them in difficult places.

Quite often when the shepherd was traveling through the valley of the shadow, it became necessary to move to another ledge of rock. The sheep may have been weak or helpless, so the shepherd used his staff to support the sheep by getting in under the legs and bringing them steadily up to the other ledge. It made a support and stabilized them. Notice Psalm 23 said, "Thy rod and thy staff, they comfort me." The rod is the Word of God. But the staff is the Holy Spirit. They both comfort me.

The word comfort in the Bible means helper. It means a stay, a support. The Holy Spirit of God is called The Comforter. He is your stay, and he is your support as you journey through this life as a child of God, the sheep of God's pasture.

This staff depicts Him. It exactly depicts the Holy Spirit. Who is the one that puts you together in unity, the unity of the spirit? He is the one Who puts you in fellowship with each other. He binds you together. He gives you unity of the spirit and the bonds of peace. The early Christians had a common unity among them in many areas alike. The Holy Spirit produced it. They had all things common, all things. There was a unity in every area of their life, brought about by the Spirit of God, (Acts 2:44). He comes therefore to bring that about in our lives. This is why he is called The Comforter. He also does another thing. He is the one that guides the children of God. He is the only one that does. You cannot be guided without him. Jesus, in John's Gospel, said, "But the Comforter, which is the Holy Ghost, whom my Father will send in my name, he shall teach you all things" (John 14:26). Just like the shepherd used his staff to keep his sheep in line to get through dangerous places, He guides us in the paths of righteousness for His name's sake. So the Spirit guides you.

He guides you in all the things of God. He guides you into the Word of God. That is why they are together here. You cannot separate them. You cannot understand the Word of God; you cannot use it unless the Holy Spirit guides you into it. That is why the staff and rod are bound together. The Word of God and the Holy Spirit are bound together. The Holy Spirit is the author of the Word of God and, being the author, He is the only one that fully can make you see it, the only one that can guide you in it.

The Holy Spirit is our teacher. He guides us into all truth. The truth is the Word of God. He is the one that guides us into the truth of the Word of God. He is the one that guides us into the worship of the Lord. The Word of God says that God seeketh those who worship Him to worship in spirit, for God is spirit. We never worship without the Holy Spirit to lead us. Just like the shepherd uses his staff to guide his sheep, the Holy Spirit guides God's children. In relationship to the Lord Jesus, He is the one that guides you into intimate fellowship with Jesus. I find when the Holy Spirit has the right position, and control over my life, Jesus becomes more precious. He has to be meaningful. Did you know you cannot make Jesus meaningful to yourself? Have you sometimes gone a day or two and have not thought of Jesus? You said, "My, I have got to change that. In the morning I am going to start off, and I am going to think about Him, and I am going to remember Him," and sure enough you forgot about Him all day long.

The Holy Spirit of God is the only one who can call you in closer to Jesus Christ. Then I know also that it is the Holy Spirit of God that liberates you, sets you free. Where the Spirit of the Lord is, there is liberty, a glorious liberty. It is glorious to be free. The Holy Spirit of God can make you free. Thank the Lord for His liberty.

The shepherd has a rod and a staff. Why both of them? The rod is for the enemies of the sheep, namely it is a weapon of warfare and protection. But the staff is mainly for the sheep, for restraint, discipline and restoration. The Word of God speaks at length about the rod and the staff in the Zechariah 11. You will find out the shepherds used them. Zechariah gave them names, Beauty and Bands. The word Beauty carries the idea of graciousness. The word Bands means unity. The word Beauty has the element of grace. There is unity.

A shepherd has to work that way. He has to work in grace and graciousness toward his sheep. They are so dumb, apt to stray, weak - they just do not know how to get on by themselves. The shepherd has to be a gracious man to put up with them. Therefore he acts in grace towards them through the beautiful Word of God. They said of Jesus the first time He preached, that His words were full of grace (Luke 4:22 and John 1:14). The shepherd acts in grace toward stray, helpless, weak, dumb sheep. A sheep is the dumbest animal in the world. You cannot train it to be in a circus to save your life. Oh how gracious is our Lord, Jesus. The Great and Good Shepherd deals with us in grace. We are just as dumb as the sheep, when it comes to things of the Spirit, we are helpless; we are guilty. We have all gone astray like sheep and he has to use the rod of Beauty on us, the Word of God, in grace. Then He also has to use the staff of Bands, unity. He is the one who by His grace binds us to Himself and to each other by the blessed Holy Spirit of God.

Curtiss F. Lee, TH. B., TH. D.

Chapter Five

THE SHEPHERD'S INSTRUMENTS (continued)

The Lord is my shepherd; I shall not want. He maketh me to lie down in green pastures. He leadeth me beside the still waters. He restoreth my soul. He leadeth me in the paths of righteousness for his name's sake. Yea, though I walk through the valley of the shadow of death, I will fear no evil: for thou art with me; thy rod and thy staff, they comfort me. Thou preparest a table before me in the presence mine enemies: thou anointest my head with oil; my cup runneth over. Surely goodness and mercy shall follow me all the days of my life: and I will dwell in the house of the Lord for ever. (Psalm 23)

Notice verse 4 said, "thy rod and thy staff they comfort me." In this section we are dealing with the shepherd's instruments, his supplies, and his equipment. In the last chapter we talked about the two instruments mentioned in Psalm 23 - the rod and the staff. But there are other instruments found elsewhere in the Bible that the shepherd had with him continually as he took care of the sheep in those open ranges, facing everything that was difficult and hard. All these instruments were necessary to do the things for the sheep as set out in this psalm. Some may not be as essential as others, but I am going to give you all of them in this one chapter, including something of their meaning and their use.

I. THE REED FLUTE

Matthew 12:20 - "A bruised reed shall he not break . . . " This speaks of a cane reed that grew in that country. Sometimes the shepherd would find a reed knocked over by an animal, and broken or blown down by the wind or something. He would cut it off and make a flute out of it. One end stopped at the joint, to make the holes for the mouthpiece. The shepherd could blow on that end and whistle.

The shepherd could make music with that reed. I am quite sure David played many of the psalms this way. When the shepherd was in the midst of some difficulty, such as when the sheep would get frightened or excited, he would softly play some quieting music on it. He especially made use of it when the sheep were lying down in the shade somewhere. The shepherd could get them settled so they would chew the cud in rhythm by playing for them. Early American cowhands practiced this same thing with cattle, and still do today.

There was nothing that pleased a shepherd as much as to see his sheep chewing their cud, all of them together. He knew they were satisfied. Chewing the cud also meant they were producing four vital products - flesh, fat, fleece and good milk.

If they did not chew their cud, he knew something was wrong with them. They would not get fat, their flesh was not going to be good, their fleece was not going to grow, and they were not going to produce any milk for the lambs. So he used the reed to play music. I am quite sure he also did it to entertain himself. He liked music. David especially liked music. He was the great musician of the Bible. At one time when he was king, he had more than 6000 musicians. He taught them all he knew about music. He is the writer of most of the Psalms, including this great 23rd Psalm.

The Psalms were the songs and music of ancient Israel. The book of Psalms is a hymnbook (or really, five of them put together). Psalms is the only hymnbook in the Bible, but it is more than that. It is a book of hymns and prayers of the saints of God. The flute was one of their main musical instruments, and David, as well the other shepherds, used it to soothe the sheep, and make them be at rest.

Music is tremendously important in life, in the lives of all of us. If you listen to cheap music, you will be like the music you listen to. It will affect you. Music has tremendous power, and the shepherd knew music had power over sheep. The shepherd put music in their lives by taking his reed flute with him, using it for their benefit even at the time of resting and chewing their cud, to quiet them when they were excited and restless.

II. THE SCRIP

The shepherd also had a bag, called a scrip. In I Samuel, Chapter 17 we find that when David the shepherd came from tending the sheep to visit his brothers, he had his bag or his scrip with him. And he put it to good use in his fight with Goliath, the giant. I Samuel 17:40 says, "And he took his staff in his hand, and chose him five smooth stones out of the brook, and put them in the shepherd's bag which he had, even in a scrip; and his sling was in his hand: and he drew near to the Philistine." And as we all know, David prevailed.

So David had his bag or scrip; the shepherds all carried one. This bag was made from the skin of a kid of the goats. It was a bag in which the shepherd put his necessary belongings - his food and all the supplies he needed to take care of the sheep on their journey. The shepherd carried it with him always.

III. THE OIL

The shepherd also carried a bottle of oil. This bottle was also made from the skin of a kid goat. But it was shaped like a bottle, and the shepherd put oil in it. The shepherd carried different kinds of oil - not only the fine beaten oil that he used for light, and the oil to apply to the sheep's head, but also other types of oil.

In the Bible we find that oil is the most consistent type of the Holy Spirit. When it is used as a necessity it always symbolizes the Holy Spirit.

Notice the shepherd's oil for a moment – how the shepherd used it. Whenever the shepherd would take his sheep to a pasture of grass where he wanted his sheep to graze, the shepherd did not lead the sheep onto the grass at first. The shepherd walked on first by himself. If there were any wasps or poisonous weeds, he would take his rod and beat them down and get them out of the way. Then if there were beasts in the middle of all these wasps, he would drive those beasts out. But there was something else he was looking for. He was looking for the viper hole. There were a lot of vipers in the pastures of the Holy Land. If a viper bit a sheep, it would die quickly. There was no cure.

So the shepherd would go throughout the grass to find the viper's hole. When he found the viper's hole, he would take his oil and pour it around and into the hole, and run it down on the inside of the hole. Then when the viper's hole was slick with oil, the shepherd would lead his sheep onto the grass. That was the method of using the oil when vipers were present. There was a two-fold purpose in using the oil this way.

1. First of all, it was Preventive. Whenever the shepherd put the oil on the edge of that hole, and it ran down the sides, when the sheep would graze close to that hole, the viper could not get up where it could strike because it could not crawl over that oil. It would slip back, and it could not strike the sheep. So the oil prevented the viper from biting the sheep. The oil was also for Protective purposes.

2. The sheep would smell that oil and move away from the hole; it was nasty smelling. They were protected in that way. Vipers in the Bible are demons. They symbolize demons. A serpent symbolizes the devil, but vipers are demons. Therefore we have a beautiful picture of the Holy Spirit of God, preventing demons from harming us and warning us of their presence. The Holy Spirit works like that. So the function of the Holy Spirit is pictured in the oil.

IV. THE SLING

The shepherd had to have these three instruments – the reed, the scrip and the oil. But there are others in the Word of God as well. One is the sling. Not only did David use his sling to fell Goliath in I Samuel, Chapter 17, but other warriors in the Word put the sling to good use. II Chronicles 26:14, speaking of King Uzziah preparing his army for battle, says, "And Uzziah prepared for them throughout all the host shields, and spears, and helmets, and habergeons, and bows, and slings to cast stones." The sling was a proven weapon for the army.

We need to know something about slings. Whenever a man knew how to use one, not only did he have his natural strength, but he had added strength in that sling. It moved with tremendous force and power. Have you ever thought about old Goliath, nine feet tall, running toward David and David toward him? When that stone hit him, it stopped his force coming toward David and knocked him down and stretched him out nine feet in his tracks. It was quite a powerful force. David had learned how to use the sling. He knew how to use it so well that he could knock out a giant with it.

A. THERE WERE SEVERAL USES OF A SLING.

1.   It was a weapon of Conflict. The shepherd had to have it. If he saw a bear coming, slipping through towards the flock, he would watch, get a good shot at him, and stop him long before he got to the sheep. There was also the lion. He did not allow the lion to come close to his sheep. He would hit him with his sling at a distance, so that he could kill him. He also used his sling on the wolves or the thieves and robbers. Whatever danger appeared, the shepherd could put one of those smooth stones in his sling and hurl it with deadly force. It was a weapon of conflict.

2.   The sling was also a weapon of Control. Sometimes, a shepherd did not have sheep dogs; he could not afford to own them. And it was difficult taking care of sheep in an open place anyway, where other shepherds had their sheep. But to control his sheep, the shepherd would look back every once in a while at his file line, his grazing line. With 100 sheep it could be a good distance back to the last one. Sometimes he would see one going astray. He would take that sling and throw a rock just the other side of the direction the sheep was going, and arrest its attention, to stop it. Then that sheep would turn around, and sometimes it would start the other way, run a little too far away from the file line. Then the shepherd would drop another stone on that side of

it. That is "goodness and mercy" as found in Psalm 23:6. That's what it is: goodness and mercy. If the shepherd did not have sheep dogs, he controlled his sheep with his sling.

3.   The shepherd also Corrected his sheep with his sling. If a sheep was unruly, he knew how hard to throw it to sting the sheep. The shepherd could just tap that sheep with a rock from his sling and make it pay attention. So it was also an instrument for correcting the sheep. In all its uses, the sling symbolizes the Holy Spirit.

The sling is not in the Bible by accident. Everything in the Bible has a spiritual meaning. The sling gave a man power beyond his natural strength, beyond human strength. It gave him a strength that he did not have by himself. Whenever he used it, he had added strength beyond his own. Remember what Paul said in II Corinthians 3:5, "Not that we are sufficient to think any thing as of ourselves; but our sufficiency is of God." The Holy Spirit came to give us power beyond our power (Acts 1:8). He is the one that faces the enemies for us. To be full of the Spirit means to be under His control.

V. THE LAMP

The shepherd always carried a lamp. It helped him at night. He did not have a flashlight like we have, or any of the big electric lights we have. He needed a lamp or a light, so he carried one with him. This lamp had a shade sort of like a Chinese lantern, made from material like parchment. Fixed in that parchment shade was a vessel, about 14 inches long. It was circular, and fastened inside. In that vessel was oil, and in that oil was a fleece wick, dipped in the oil. When the shepherd lit the fleece, the oil gave him light.

This was a very important instrument, because the shepherd did much of his work at night, most importantly, counting and inspecting the sheep after he brought them to the fold in the nighttime. Sometimes he had to go after one that was missing. The shepherd always had his lamp with him.

The shepherd's lamp is found in Psalm 119:105. "Thy word is a lamp unto my feet and a light unto my path." In that scripture we can see a two-fold use of the lamp. First is the light to the shepherd's feet. He would sit down sometimes at nighttime and put the lamp between his feet at to warm them. When he went down a pathway, he could shine it on the pathway in front of him and see whatever was down the pathway. David learned this being a shepherd. It is not any problem to find out what light symbolizes in the Bible. You do not have to guess; it is right in this scripture.

The light of God's Word has several uses.

1. First of all, it gives illumination. Psalm 119:130 says, "The entrance of thy word giveth light . . . " It gives man understanding, discernment, and the power of perception. It enables the shepherd to see down the pathway things that he could not see otherwise. God illuminates us with His Word. He gives us wisdom beyond the natural. He gives a perception to students of the Bible that others do not have.

2. The lamp is also an instrument of revelation. The shepherd's lamp revealed what was on the pathway. He could turn his light down a pathway and see the eyes of different beasts, and temporarily blind them. Yes, light blinds, but it let the shepherd see. He found out what was down the path by revelation. The Bible is the revelation of God, or God revealing Himself and His will to us. The Word of God is sealed, and no revelation goes beyond it. So the lamp is an instrument of revelation.

3. The lamp is an instrument of animation. It will warm your soul. The shepherd's feet could be cold and almost asleep, with no blood circulating. He would place the lamp between his feet, warm his feet, the blood would flow, and his feet would come alive.

The Word will warm you up in two ways:

1. Somtimes it warms you up by making you mad. That shows you are not dead when you get mad. You are still alive. There is hope for you. Jeremiah said in Jeremiah 20:9, " . . . But his word was in my

heart as a burning fire shut up in my bones." He had to speak it forth against those who were against him, trying to restrain him; he couldn't help himself.

2. Sometimes it warms you by filling you with joy. In Luke, Chapter 24, Jesus spoke to two of His followers after His resurrection, but they did not recognize Him at first. When they did, in Luke 24:32, one of them said, " . . . Did not our heart burn within us while he talked with us by the way, and while he opened to us the scriptures?" They were warmed by the Living Word of God. Read His Word; it will warm your soul.

   A. The lamp is also an instrument of restoration. When the shepherd made his sheep pass under the rod to enter the fold, if one was missing, he let the porter take over, lit that lamp, and went looking for that lamb to restore it. The only way to restore our fellowship with God is with the Word of God. "He restoreth my soul."

   B. The lamp is also an instrument of correction. We know it is light that pierces the darkness, that corrects and reproves us. Hebrews 4:12 says, "For the word of God is quick and powerful, and sharper than any two-edged sword . . ."

What gives the lamp its ability to serve so many functions? Obviously, it is the oil that is within it. The lamp is of no use to the shepherd without the oil. The Word of God is just like a lamp unlighted to us, unless the Holy Spirit of God activates it and makes it real to us. We cannot separate the two.

So when we have a lamp, oil is necessary. It is just a dead book without it. God's Word is only understood, when the oil (The Holy Spirit) is there as well. The oil is the Holy Spirit illuminating the Word of God to us. And unless the Holy Spirit of God activates it and makes it real to us. We cannot separate the two. And it's the Holy Spirit Who makes the Word sharper than any two-edged sword, to give direction to our lives. (Hebrews

4:12)

VI. THE GARMENT

The other instrument really isn't an instrument, but I will call it one for the purpose of this study. It is a garment. It is not normally called an instrument, but it served as one for the shepherd. The shepherd's garment was an outward robe or a coat. It covered his other clothes. This garment was made of sheep's skin and fleece. The first time it is mentioned was in the Garden of Eden when God clothed Adam and Eve in skin. God killed a sheep, took the skin off and clothed Adam and Eve. (Genesis 3:21) The garment was just the skin, with the fleece still on it. Killing that sheep was how God taught Adam and Eve about the altar, the blood and the sacrifice, that they taught their sons.

So God clothed the first humans in sheepskin, with fleece on it. Shepherds wear their garments both ways (fleece side in and fleece side out) in the Holy Land, because the climate there is variable.

In the daytime, especially in summer, it is extremely hot. At night it gets very cold. In fact, can be 100 degrees difference in temperature in some areas between the daytime and the nighttime.

The shepherd would place the fleece next to him to stay warm at night. Then he would turn the white wool to the outside and put the skin against him in the daytime. The skin has oil in it that keeps the heat from penetrating, which makes it cooler. In an automobile, if the top is white, it stays about 15 percent cooler. The white fleece reflects the heat, and wool is the whitest thing we know. It gets rid of the heat.

The shepherd also used the garment in another way. The garment was used by the shepherd to show his relationship to the sheep. That garment of wool provided identification with the sheep. He looked like them, and smelled like them. He identified with them.

What did the Lord Jesus Christ do, the Good Shepherd do? He came and identified Himself with us. The Bible says He took it upon himself, the likeness of man. He looked like us and smelled like us, and was subject to our same human frailities. Christ identified Himself with us, His children, the sheep of his pasture, just as the shepherd did when he put on the sheepskin garment. He wanted to be identified with the sheep.

Not only was it a matter of identification; it also was protection. The shepherd was protected against the heat and the cold of the weather. And sometimes he would find a sickly, cold, wet sheep. The shepherd would take that sheep and turn the wool inside on his garment, put that sheep in the wool, and keep it in his bosom. When they came to the fold that night, if that sheep was not better, he would lie down with that sheep wrapped up in that coat with him, with the wool touching it, and get it good and warm, so that his heat contributed to the heat of the sheep. By morning, it was restored.

But the garment has another use; it is a coat of propitiation. The shepherd acquired his fleece coat, that covering, by shedding blood; something died; a sheep died. The shepherd took that garment in love and appreciation, because the life of a sheep had been taken, its blood spilled in total propitiation. The shepherd's ragged, dirty clothes, if he had any, were covered by that garment.

He covered his nakedness with it. He covered his sheep with it when they were sickly, and when they were wet and cold. You know what that sheep covering represents? It represents the righteousness of Jesus: being clothed in His righteousness by His blood, total propitiation. We are never clothed in the righteousness of Jesus until we come under the blood of Jesus.

This is not a full list of the shepherd's instruments, but it explains the meanings, or the significance, of the most important of them.

Chapter Six

THE SHEPHERD'S RELATIONSHIP TO THE SHEEP

"Thou Art With Me"

The Lord is my shepherd. I shall not want. He maketh me to lie down in green pastures. He leadeth me beside the still waters. He restoreth my soul. He leadeth me in the paths of righteousness for his name's sake. Yea, though I walk through the valley of the shadow of death, I will fear no evil for though art with me; thy rod and thy staff they comfort me. Thou preparest a table before me in the presence of mine enemies. Thou anointest my head with oil, my cup runneth over. Surely goodness and mercy shall follow me all the days of my life, and I will dwell in the house of the Lord forever. (Psalm 23)

Verily, verily, I say unto you, he that entereth not by the door into the sheepfold, but climbeth up some other way, the same is a thief and a robber. But he that entereth in by the door is the shepherd of the sheep. To him the porter openeth; and the sheep hear his voice: and he calleth his own sheep by name, and leadeth them out. And when he putteth forth his own sheep, he goeth before them, and the sheep follow him: for they know his voice. And a stranger will they not follow, but will flee from him, for they know not the voice of strangers. This parable spake Jesus unto them; but they understood not what things they were which he spake unto them. Then said Jesus unto them again, Verily, verily, I say unto you, I am the door of the sheep. All that ever came before me are thieves and robbers; but the sheep did not hear them. I am the door; by me if any man enter in, he shall be saved and shall go in and out and find pasture. The thief cometh not, but for to steal, and to kill, and to destroy: I am come that they might have life, and that they might have it more abundantly. I am the good shepherd: the good shepherd giveth his life for the sheep. But he that is an hireling, and not the shepherd, whose own the sheep are not, seeth the wolf coming, and leaveth the sheep, and fleeth: and the wolf catcheth them, and scattereth the sheep. The hireling fleeth, because he is an hireling, and careth not for the sheep. I am the good shepherd, and know my sheep, and am known of mine. As the Father knoweth me, even so know I the Father; and I lay down my life for the sheep. And other sheep I have, which are not of this fold: them also I must bring, and they shall hear my voice: and there shall be one fold, and one shepherd. Therefore, doth my Father love me, because I laid down my life, that I might take it again. No man taketh it from me, but that I lay it down of myself. I have power to lay it down, and I have power to take it again. This commandment have I received of my Father. (John 10:1-18)

Then came the Jews round about him, and said unto him, How long dost thou make us to doubt? If thou be the Christ, tell us plainly. Jesus answered them, I told you, and ye believed not; the works that I do in my Father's name, they bear witness of me. But ye believe not, because ye are not of my sheep, as I said unto you. My sheep hear my voice, and I know them, and they follow me: and I give unto them eternal life; and they shall never perish, neither shall any man pluck them out of my hand.
My Father, which gave them me, is greater than all; and no man is able to pluck them out of my Father's hand. I and my Father are one. John 10:24-30

You will not find in the Scripture a better description of the relationship that exists between a shepherd and his sheep than these verses. That is the shepherd of the Holy Land and the sheep of the Holy Land. We do not have anything like this in the western world. We put sheep in a pasture, put up a fence; we try to fix it so that animals and dogs cannot get through. They are left alone. But not in the Holy Land.

The shepherd has a very vital relationship to his sheep all the time. Psalm 23 puts an emphasis on the relationship between the shepherd and his sheep. "The Lord is my shepherd. I shall not want." He had to provide all the provisions. "He maketh me lie down in green pastures. He leadeth me beside the still waters. He restoreth my soul. He leadeth me in the paths of righteousness for his name's sake." And then the pronoun changes as if David was talking to the shepherd. "Yea, though I walk through the valley of the shadow of death, . . . thou art with me." Not "he" but "thou", just like talking to somebody face-to-face. "Thy rod and thy staff they comfort me." David is showing us the shepherd's relationship to the sheep. In John, Chapter 10 that is what Jesus was talking about. What He as the Good Shepherd does for His people, who are called the sheep of His pasture.

In these scriptures, as well as many other places in the Bible, we can find the shepherd fulfilling his relationship to the sheep.

I. THE SHEPHERD FINDS THE SHEEP

The shepherd's relationship with the sheep begins with finding them. Jesus said in the Scripture, "Other sheep I have . . . them also I must bring" (John 10:16). In Luke, Chapter 15, it says that if a shepherd has a hundred sheep and discovers that one is missing, he goes out until he finds it, lays it on his shoulders, and brings that which was lost home. You will find emphasis throughout Scripture on the shepherd finding the sheep. I do not know anything, except a human, that can get as helplessly and hopelessly lost as a sheep. It is hard to lose a dog, a cat, or even a horse. They will find their way back. You cannot lose cattle. They will get there. But sheep can be so lost, they have no sense of ever getting back. They are helplessly and hopelessly lost when they go astray.

Just think about the lost-ness of sheep. First of all, think about the ways a sheep is lost.

1. A sheep is lost Heedlessly. A sheep will look and see a blade of grass, pull out of line away from the flock, and nibble that piece of

grass without taking heed of what it is doing. It will reach and get another. The first thing you know, it is totally separated from the flock and the shepherd, and goes farther and farther away. It is heedless of any sort of danger. It does not know there is danger from the lion, the bear, the wolves, scavenger dogs and the robbers and thieves. Danger is ever present when the sheep is away from the shepherd. The Bible very plainly teaches us this is exactly like man who is lost. He is heedlessly lost. He does not sense the danger. He does not know his lost condition. He does not understand. He does not see it. A man is heedlessly lost until the Holy Spirit convicts him of that. Jesus said in John 6:44, "No man can come to me, except the Father which hath sent me draw him . . ." The prodigal son had a great time by himself for a while. He had a high old time. He went away from his father, had money, everybody played up to him, until he became bankrupt. His father was looking for him because the scripture says in Luke 15:20, " . . . when he was yet a great way off, his father saw him, and had compassion, and ran , and fell on his neck and kissed him." Lost men are like that, heedlessly lost.

2. A sheep is Senselessly lost. A sheep has no sense or awareness of its lostness. A sheep does not understand how to get back to the shepherd and the flock. The more it tries, the more lost it becomes, and the more confused it becomes. A sheep does not see well, it does not hear well, it is in flight, it has no power, or resistance, or defense. It is just senselessly lost. It has no sense of direction, it cannot find its way at all. That is how men are lost. They are lost just exactly like a sheep, senselessly lost. They do not know their way. They do not know their condition. They do not understand. In Matthew, chapter 13, Jesus describes them as having ears that hear not, eyes that see not, and a heart that understands not. That is how sheep and men are lost.

3. A sheep is Defenselessly lost. A sheep cannot defend itself. It has no way to fight back. It will not even try. Let an animal come after it - it will not bleat, it will not fight back, it will not try to strike, it does

not know how. It will not run. Left alone, a little old dog can get after one, and it will not run far before it will lie down, and let the dog come and cut its throat. It is defenselessly lost. It is helpless against the enemy. It cannot defend itself. We do not like to think this, but men are lost like that. They have no way in the world to defend themselves against the devil and the demons and the power of the enemies of their souls. Men just cannot defend against them. Men are just as helpless and lost as a sheep, with no defense against the evil forces of this world. When they are lost in sin, men are captured in the hand of the devil and in slavery to sin. The world system controls and men are defenseless against it. II Timothy 2:24-26 says, "And the servant of the Lord must not strive; but be gentle unto all men, apt to teach, patient, In meekness instructing those that oppose themselves; if God peradventure will give them repentance to the acknowledging of the truth; AND THAT THEY MAY RECOVER THEMSELVES OUT OF THE SNARE OF THE DEVIL, WHO ARE TAKEN CAPTIVE BY HIM AT HIS WILL".

Without the strength to repent that comes from God, men are defenseless. So sheep and men are defenselessly lost. That is what it means to be lost. In the Scripture when a sheep is lost it means separation - separation from the shepherd, separation from the flock, separation from the fold. It is separated. The Bible speaks about three kinds of death: physical, spiritual and eternal. Every one of them involves a type of separation.

1. Physical death. James said that " . . . the body without the spirit is dead . . . " (James 2:26). A separation. That is really what happens to us when the spirit and soul take their departure from the body; the body is just dead. Life's gone from it. It is dead. That's the separation that takes place.

2. Spiritual death. There is also the matter of spiritual death, a different type of separation. It means that a person is separated from his source of life, GOD IN JESUS CHRIST. God gives life to men in Christ. When a man does not believe in him, he is separated from the

source of life; therefore he is spiritually dead. That is a separation.

3. Eternal death. This is a separation that has no remedy. There is a sense in which lost sinners are not separated totally from God. God is everywhere, and men can find Him in all areas of life, for He is seeking them. They receive many blessings from God. He sends rain and sunshine upon the lost. Jude described the lost as a wandering star - a star separated from place, separated from a period in time, separated from everything. Separation also means non-responsiveness. While the sheep is separated from the shepherd, it cannot respond to the shepherd. There is no responsiveness. It cannot respond to the flock. It cannot respond to the fold. Eternal death is non-responsive. A dead man cannot respond. Lost man just does not have any response to God.

Evangelists will say to their audiences, "You come on, come to Jesus, you get up and come on, you make your way down, you determine your eternal destiny. You choose." A man who is dead in trespasses and sin has to have someone to find him. When a sheep was lost, Jesus said the shepherd had to find it. Lost also means impaired or endangered. Any lost sheep in the Holy Land in Jesus' time was in grave danger from lions, bears, wolves, scavenger dogs, vipers and everything else that would destroy him. That is why a shepherd would leave every sheep he had in the fold and go in haste and with anxiety, hurrying to find the lost sheep. It was gravely impaired.

Jesus said, " . . . fear him which is able to destroy both soul and body in hell" (Matthew 10:28). Jesus came to rescue man from eternal death. That is what it means to be lost. The sheep never finds the shepherd. The shepherd has to find the sheep. Everywhere in the Bible, you will find that if someone gets saved, it is because Jesus has gone after him.

I have heard some people say, "I found God." They did not find God. Romans 3:11 says, " . . . there is none that seeketh after God." The shepherd has to find the sheep where it is and as it is, lost. It is in a lost state when he finds it. If God starts on your trail, He will find you. He does not start out and then quit. He seeks till He finds that which is lost.

The difference between Christianity and all the other religions of the world is in the person of Jesus, the only one who died, rose again, and lives forever. The founders of the other religions died and they are still dead. They cannot compare to Jesus. He is incomparable. There is nobody like Him. He stands alone. Christianity is a relationship; everything else is just a religion. The other religions in this world began with man seeking God. But they say that man is good; he wants God so much that he just keeps on till he finds him, their false god. The Bible says man does not seek after God, and cannot because he is dead in trespasses and sin.

The first man, Adam, sinned and became lost. We need to look at that carefully because it has all the fundamentals. When Adam and Eve sinned against God, God came searching for them; they did not run to find Him. They ran and hid from Him. They had grown afraid of God. Lost man does not want God, even though He sent His Son down from heaven to seek and to save that which was lost. Once the Holy Spirit starts convicting man, then he will seek God. But God already has sought Him first. The Bible says He loved us first. We love Him because He first loved us. That is the divine order.

A young man was saved and was asked by an old puritan how it came about. He said, "Well, God did His part and I did my part." The puritan said, "What was your part?" the young man answered, truthfully, "to run from God just as hard as I could until He ran me down and caught me." That is what God has to do. He has to run us down. The shepherd has to go hunting for that stray and lost sheep. The sheep will never find itself; it will never come back on its own. It does not even know it is lost. It can get swallowed up by a lion or get tangled in the thorns, thistles, briers, bushes, and just hang there by its wool. The shepherd goes after it until he finds that which is lost. Jesus said, "other sheep I have, which are not of this fold, them also I must bring . . . " (John 10:16). There is a difference between Christianity and the natural religion of man. Dead sinners cannot come to Christ on their own. They have to be found by the Good Shepherd.

II. THE SHEPHERD FOALS THE SHEEP

That means the shepherd gives life to them. Jesus said, "And I give unto them eternal life; and they shall never perish . . ." (John 10:28) This concept holds true throughout the natural world. There has to be seed; there has to be pollination. There has to be the female and the male relationship. Even in vegetation - flowers and things like that - there is a pollination that must precede a birth. Nothing comes into this world without a birth of some kind. If you have physical life, you have it by birth. If you have spiritual life, you have it by spiritual birth.

How does Jesus give eternal life? He gives it by <u>spiritual</u> birth. That is why you must be born again. Did you know the shepherd controlled the birth of the lambs? He knew the season. He brought about physical life to them, and so it is in the realm of the spiritual for us. God alone can beget you, and give you a spiritual birth. The Bible says you must be born of God. We cannot give ourselves physical life or spiritual life. That is why Jesus said in John 3:6, "That which is born of the flesh is flesh; and that which is born of the Spirit is spirit." Speaking of those who receive Jesus as their Lord and Savior, John says in John 1:13, "Which were born, not of blood, nor of the will of flesh, nor of the will of man, but of God." That eliminates everybody except God from giving you spiritual birth.

Our natural or physical birth comes through our parents. That is our background, our lineage. Our parents could not give us spiritual birth. They could give us physical birth, but not spiritual birth. There is no other man that can give spiritual birth. Pope, priest, pastor, parents, preachers - it does matter: no one else can give spiritual birth. That is why water baptism is not essential to spiritual birth because that is something a man does for us. If it were essential, man would not have anything to do with it (not by the will of man). So if water baptism was essential to spiritual birth, a preacher could either damn you or save you. He could refuse to baptize you. You would die in your sin and be separated from God eternally.

This matter of spiritual birth is of God. It cannot be any other way. God though Jesus Christ gives us spiritual birth and brings eternal life. So the Good Shepherd foals the sheep. He has to give us life. He foals us. Gives us the birth that brings us into the family of God, where we have eternal life.

III. THE SHEPHERD FEEDS THE SHEEP.

Not only does the shepherd foal the sheep, he also feeds the sheep. "He maketh me to lie down in green pastures. He leadeth me beside the still waters . . . Thou preparest a table before me in the presence of mine enemies: My cup runneth over." This is the shepherd's mode of feeding the sheep. He knows where the pastures are. He leads them there. He knows where the water is. He leads them there. He knows how to prepare the table for them.

In the Holy Land the shepherd had to hunt for grass. Many times in a shady place of a mountain, away from the tableland, he found grass growing, the most luscious and fine grass, because it had been shaded against the heat of the summer, from the hot, eastern sun. When the shepherd found it, there might be poisonous weeds growing in that grass. In that grass also there could be viper holes. A shepherd never led the sheep right into that grass. The shepherd went first while the sheep stood and looked on. He prepared a table before them in the presence of their enemies. The shepherd beat out the poisonous weeds and put oil on the viper holes so the sheep could safely come and eat. Whenever the shepherd thought it was ready, he would lead them to the wonderful grass and let them graze to their fill. He prepared a table.

The table God spreads for us is the Word of God. What else can we feed on for spiritual food? A sheep is a clean-natured animal and will not eat anything unclean. An old goat is not clean in nature. He will eat the filthiest thing in the world. An old goat will eat that which a hog will not eat. The hog will eat every thing except a cigar butt. An old goat will come along and pick up a cigar butt, chew it up and enjoy it. The sheep likes only that which is clean. So the shepherd feeds it on a clean table. He feeds them on that which is luscious green grass. A well-fed sheep will lie down and chew its cud, while a hungry sheep is restless. It will not lie down. It just cannot be content and rest until its hunger is met.

The people of God's pasture cannot feed on junk and have their spirit satisfied, either. This generation of Christians is trying to satisfy their children, this generation of young people, with materialism. We have a hungry generation of youth, starved for spiritual food. They are not going to the green pastures because the pastures have not been prepared properly by the under shepherd (pastor or priest) to feed the sheep.

IV. THE SHEPHERD FOREGOES THE SHEEP.

Jesus said, when the shepherd "putteth forth his own sheep, he goeth before them" (John 10:4). David said, " . . .he leadeth me beside the still waters. He restoreth my soul: he leadeth me in the paths of righteousness." Whenever a shepherd took his sheep from the fold, he never drove them to pasture. He led them. He always went before them.

Quite often, in the Holy Land in the early morning, maybe about 3AM because the sun comes up there earlier than it does here in North America, the shepherd will take his place and call his sheep by name and they come to him. Each one has a place in line, a grazing line, what we may call a file line. They have their place. They do not get out of place. There is always a lead sheep. That one will come first and stand right next to the shepherd, then the next one and the next one and next one, until they are all in line. They take their places in the early morning and start right off toward the place of grazing.

They need to graze before the hot sun is up, while the dew is still on the grass. They get a drink besides food from the grass. The shepherd leads them. He goes before them. He even goes down into the valley of the shadow of the death first. He faces everything first. He is out ahead of them. He never leaves them to get somewhere by themselves. He leads them to wherever they go.

A shepherd will never allow his sheep in the Holy Land to make a journey by themselves. A shepherd could not do it. He would not be a shepherd if he did. The sheep could not get back to the fold that night. Most of them would be killed before the day was gone. So a shepherd goes before them.

Nothing ever takes him by surprise. He knows the end from the beginning. He knows every difficult place he has to go and he actually knows the way through the valley of the shadow of death. Jesus, our Great Shepherd, said He would never leave us and God never has.

Moses led the children of Israel. Do you know how he learned everything about that wilderness? He was a shepherd there for 40 years. Did you know he had to practice leading sheep for 40 years in that same wilderness where he led the Israelites for 40 years? He knew every sheep track. He knew every one of them. He knew where to go for water. He knew where the grass was. He knew everything about the "waste howling wilderness" (Deuteronomy 32:10). He led the children of Israel for 40 years there. Moses was a great prophet and a great shepherd. For 40 years he shepherded sheep, and for another 40 years he shepherded God's people. He carried them through everything.

It was a land full of false shepherds and scorpions. Moses knew where all that was. He knew what a "waste howling wilderness" was. He knew it was a terrible one because he lived there 40 years before. He knew the serpents and the vipers were there. He knew the wild beasts were there. He had faced them before. Moses started out leading them and, of course, God brought them through. God did not leave Israel to get through the wilderness for 40 years by themselves. They would have got lost in it. They all could have died without getting through it.

Jesus Christ our Great and Good Shepherd says, I will never leave you nor forsake you. He is not going to leave you to try and get through the waste howling wilderness of this world alone. We could not and would not get through this world without our Great Shepherd going before us.

Jesus Christ is our Good, Great, Chief Shepherd and He will bring us to His Father's House, that fold where all the sheep of God's pasture are destined to live eternally.

Curtiss F. Lee, TH. B., TH. D.

Chapter Seven

THE SHEPHERD'S RELATIONSHIP TO THE SHEEP (CONTINUED)

The Lord is my shepherd. I shall not want. He maketh me to lie down in green pastures. He leadeth me beside the still waters. He restoreth my soul. He leadeth me in the path of righteousness for his name's sake." (Psalm 23:1-3)

Last chapter I wrote about four aspects of the shepherd's relationship to his sheep. First, he finds the sheep. I would like for you to remember that no sheep ever, ever found the shepherd. The shepherd must search for and go after them, and he does. Second, he feeds the sheep. Third, he foals the sheep; he gives life unto them. Jesus said, "I give unto them eternal life." That life comes by spiritual birth. Fourth, he foregoes or leads the sheep. When he puts forth his sheep, he goes before them to make sure they will be safe.

I. THE SHEPHERD FONDLES THE SHEEP

When you are showing love to sheep, or other animals, you fondle them. We do not use this word often in relationship to adults, but if you have a little baby you fondle it; that is what you say. That same idea is expressed in the Word of God, if not with exactly that word. Isaiah 40:11 says of the

Lord, "He shall feed his flock like a shepherd: he shall gather the lambs with his arm, and carry them in his bosom, and shall gently lead those that are with young."

Jesus said in John 10:11, " . . . the good shepherd giveth his life for the sheep." That means that he loves them enough that he would die for them. The shepherds have a peculiar, strong and rare love for their sheep. There is no relationship between man and any other animal anywhere in the world that compares to the love a shepherd in the Holy Land has for his sheep. There is no relationship like it.

1. The shepherd's love for the sheep is Personal. He loves each one of his sheep. He makes that love fit the nature of that particular sheep. He does not just love them as a flock, as a group together; he has a specific personal love for each one of his sheep. Christ loved me and gave Himself for me. That is a personal thing. It is something we almost have taken out of Christianity. We have made it so social we do not think much about the individual. The whole group is now what is important, not the individual. But in God's sight, it is the individual that is important. Jesus loved the person, and that means that He loves you. There are people you just cannot love the same way. You love them with the same love, but you have to love them in a different manner, because they are different in their nature. A man does not love his children in the same way he loves his grandchildren. They are different in nature. The shepherd knows that about his sheep. They are different in nature. They respond differently and he loves them personally. Jesus' love is so full and varied that it will meet my own personal needs. I just cannot take Paul's salvation and the love God had for Paul. I have to have it personally. I am a different person from Paul. So the shepherd loved his sheep individually, each one of them.

2. The shepherd's love for the sheep is Positive. It is active. He does not just love in words. He loves in actions. Everything he does for his sheep is an active expression of his love for them. It is positive

and active; that love always takes the initiative toward the sheep. The shepherd does not wait for the sheep to respond to him in love and come back to him. He steps out after it. We did not love God first; He loved us first. He took the initiative in His love towards us. He came after us in love. The Scripture said if the shepherd lost one sheep, he went after it until he found it. A shepherd constantly acted on behalf of the sheep. All day long he would take care of them. Then he would put them in the fold at night and sleep with them, sleep at the door to the sheepfold. It was a positive, active love that he had for his sheep. Our Shepherd had to take the initiative in loving us, because in our state of deadness in sins, we could not seek Him. He had to seek us. The state we were in made it necessary that He love us in a positive, initiatory way. The very nature of sin makes that necessary. Sin separates. God, through the Lord Jesus Christ, loved us with a positive love that was very initiatory and active, and continues to be. John 13:1 says, " . . . having loved his own which were in the world, he loved them unto the end." It was just a continual expression of His love in action toward those He loved. The shepherd loved his sheep in a very positive way.

3. The shepherd's love for the sheep is Proud. The shepherd had great pride in his sheep. He thought that there was nothing too good for them. Jesus said that the good shepherd gives his life for his sheep. That is exactly what it cost Him. It cost Him his life. That is a very expensive love, one that gives its best and its all. He did not just give partially. He gave of Himself totally in His love for His sheep. And He died a sacrificial death in the end.

4. The shepherd loves his sheep with a Priceless love. The shepherd's love is free and it is voluntary. The sheep did not pay a price for the love of the shepherd. Neither do we get the love of Christ by any sort of sacrifice or price we pay. It is free to us. This is one of the things that astounds me about the love of Christ. He has no selfish motives whatever. There was not anything in us that could motivate Him to love us. When He loved us, He was not trying to get

something for Himself. He loved us with the only unselfish love in this world. Our love is selfish. We see something in others we need; not so with Jesus. There is not anything in us He needs. What could we give Him that He doesn't already have? How can we improve on perfection? Without us He is still perfect. He could do totally without us and never be imperfect. He just loves with a love that is completely unselfish. The shepherd's love for his sheep never ends. He loved His own up until the end, and God said, "I love you with an eternal love." It never ends. God is eternal, of course, and Jesus is, too. The Shepherd continually loves His sheep.

This is the type of love the shepherd had and has for his sheep. I am using the word fondle to represent that because fondling an animal is an expression of love, so that is exactly what the shepherd does.

II. THE SHEPHERD FAMILIARIZES HIMSELF WITH THE SHEEP

John 10:3 says, " . . . he calleth his own sheep by name." That is more than just a theoretical knowledge of them. He gets very familiar with them and has a very intimate relationship with them. He knows their names because he gave their names to them. Some of the names are like Pure and White, Gray-eared, Black Legs, and a few other descriptive things shepherds would call them. I could not remember names for 100 sheep. I would not know them all but the shepherd did. He knew all their names exactly. I do not know how he retained them all, but he retained them all. A shepherd was good at names. He knew each one's name in a very familiar way. He had a very familiar knowledge of the nature of the sheep.

Sheep are different in their natures. They were not alike in their responses and he knew their natures. He knew how he had to deal with each sheep in order to control it. He knew everything about the nature of the sheep. He also knew the needs of the sheep. He understood their needs exactly, and he had the supplies ready to meet those needs

He knew the strengths of the sheep and the weaknesses of the sheep. He knew their proneness to wander. The psalmist said, "Lord, thou tellest my wanderings." God's children are prone to wander. They have a proneness to wander like sheep that go astray. The shepherd knew their endurance. Therefore he never pushed the sheep beyond their endurance. He knew the dangers they faced. Ever danger they had to face he knew, because he had gone before them.

Our Shepherd knows all about us also. We may deceive somebody else but not the Great Shepherd. He knows all our defects. He knows all our illnesses, all our shortcomings and all our sins. He knows all about our attitude and our spirit. He even knows our thoughts. God's Word says He knows our thoughts before we even have them. That is the kind of Shepherd we have. Saying, "I know my sheep," means more than just having information; it means having an intimate knowledge. It is experience in the knowledge of them. There is a closeness.

The shepherd examines his sheep from time to time. He will not let them go many days without an examination. If one of them shows any sign of weakness or anything that looks wrong, he quickly examines it. He knows about everything that has transpired, or is transpiring in their lives. So he keeps up with them. He familiarizes himself with his sheep.

II. THE SHEPHERD FURBISHES HIS SHEEP

There is a statement in the Scripture that tells us about it. In Song of Solomon 6:6, the bridegroom says, "Thy teeth are as a flock of sheep which go up from the washing . . .". The shepherd takes the sheep to clean water. The sheep are so constituted that their wool picks up dirt and dust and it settles in, mats up; it gets dirty and ugly looking. The shepherd will not stand that for long. He will find a good watering place and give them a good washing. He cleans them up. Our Great and Good Shepherd cleans us, too.

Our initial cleansing is by the blood. " . . . the blood of Jesus Christ His Son cleanses us from all sin" (I John 1:7). When we are saved, His blood is full and final payment for our sins. David said in Psalm 51:7, " . . . wash me and I shall be whiter than snow." The Blessed Shepherd Jesus Christ takes the blackest sin in this world and makes it whiter than snow, it says - not as white, but whiter than snow.

We know that snow is the whitest thing that man knows anything about, but this scripture says He makes us whiter than snow. It goes beyond the whiteness of the natural snow, when He washes us in the blood and cleanses us. But there is another way He cleanses, and that is continually by His Word. He cleanses not only by the blood, but also by the Book. In John 15:3, Jesus said, "Now ye are clean through the word which I have spoken unto you." The Bible also says that you are sanctified by the Word, which also means cleansed by the Word. We find in Ephesians 5:26 that He was going to sanctify the church with "the washing of water by the word."

Many times in the Bible, water represents the Word of God. That is what Jesus had in mind when He took water to wash Simon Peter's feet. Peter protested that Jesus was not going to wash his feet, no sir, Peter was too humble for that. Being proud, that was what was the matter with him. He called it humility but it was pride. He thought he didn't need washing. Jesus said, "If I wash thee not, thou hast no part with me" (John 13:8). Peter repented then, and asked Jesus to wash his hands and head as well. Our feet carry us through this world; that's how we make physical contact with it as we go. Our walk represents our manner of life. We will get our feet dirty and need to have them washed.

We live in an evil, wicked, polluted, filthy society. We need the words of the Shepherd, the basic Word of God, applied to our lives every day. He furbishes his sheep. He makes them clean and those are the two things he uses us to do it - His love and His Book, the blood of Christ and the words of the Bible. I do not know any other way He can cleanse you. So He furbishes His sheep, gets them clean by the blood and by the Word. Continuous reading of God's Word will cleanse us from the things of this world that we are exposed to.

III. THE SHEPHERD FORTIFIES HIS SHEEP

The whole 23rd Psalm talks about this. "The Lord is my Shepherd; I shall not want." That is fortification. "He maketh me to lie down in green pastures. He leadeth me beside the still waters. He restoreth my soul." That is fortifying the soul. "Yea, though I walk through the valley of the shadow of death, I will fear no evil. For thou art with me; thy rod and staff they comfort me."

The shepherd has ways to fortify his sheep in health, and to fortify them in fellowship around him. So that was what he did. He had to keep them strong. He had to keep them from becoming fearful. He fortified them by his presence.

If you want to get sheep upset and disturbed, cause them to lose their peace and calm, let their shepherd be absent. There is not a flock that will not get disturbed when the shepherd is absent. That would happen when the shepherd had to go sometimes check over the highland ahead. They would get disturbed and run off if he left them for long. They have no peace, calm and tranquility when the shepherd is absent. So he fortifies them with his presence. The shepherd knows when the sheep begin to get restless, when they begin to grow weary, when they begin to get disturbed. He will take his flute and play soothing music to calm and quiet them down. They get calm around him. And many times in time of danger when the sheep are strung out a long distance from him, a hundred of them one behind the other, they will get restless and disturbed. The smell of other animals will make them so. The shepherd will stop and corral them around him. They will all gather around close to him and settle down in quietness and not be disturbed.

The presence of the shepherd is essential. One thing that makes the Christian life so wonderful, that gives us the wonderful feeling of peace and tranquility, is the consciousness of the daily presence of Jesus Christ in our lives. If you do not have conscious fellowship with Jesus Christ, then you are a disturbed sheep. You are restless. You are not satisfied. This is what makes the Christian life a thrill – a daily walk with Jesus, in His presence. You know you're in His presence and He's in yours, if you're really having that fellowship with Him.

The shepherd fortifies the sheep with his provisions. For example, if they're hungry, the shepherd takes them to grass, because a hungry sheep gets restless. It will not lie down. It will start hunting something to eat. So the shepherd gets the table ready for them. He feeds them so they will not be restless. If they're not fed, they get poor and weak. So he gives them the provisions of food in order to make them strong. When they are thirsty, he has water ready; he leads them by the still waters.

He is the one who fortifies them with all provisions. He has provision of certain ingredients to restore them to health. He will clean them with oil and water in order to restore them. He fortifies them with his provisions. We have the provisions of Christ for our life so we too can be fortified and strengthened.

The shepherd fortifies the sheep by his passion. A shepherd has to love his sheep in order to satisfy his sheep. His sheep would not be satisfied with somebody that hates them; somebody that is boisterous, loud, rough or cruel. They would never settle down. Sheep are conscious of the love of the shepherd. The shepherd fortifies them with his time. He makes them secure. He fights off the lions, bears, wolves, scavenging dogs, keeps out the vipers, beats down the robbers, and gives them a sense of security in his strength. The Great Shepherd fortifies the sheep of His pasture with His providence, His prayers, His promises, and His people.

IV. THE SHEPHERD FEATURES HIS SHEEP

A shepherd, when his sheep are fat and their wool is fine, clean and white, loves to show them off to other shepherds. He likes for them to be seen. Matthew 25:33 says that the Good Shepherd will set His sheep on His right hand. That's the place of display in honor and glory, on His right hand. He puts those old goats on His left hand, but He displays His sheep. He likes to feature them.

That is the exact opposite of what is talked about in Hebrews 10:33 and I Corinthians 4:9. Hebrew 10:33 says, "Partly, whilst ye were made a gazingstock both by reproaches and afflictions; and partly, whilst ye became companions of them that were so used." Keep in mind this word gazingstock. Look also at the word "spectacle" in I Corinthians 4:9. " . . . for we are made a spectacle unto the world, and to angels, and to men." Notice these words "gazingstock" and "spectacle." These words are used in reference to a theater. They mean that the theater is open and there is an audience, and the actors have come on stage. They are putting on a show, but they are a joke, a mockery.

Let me tell you what God is doing. God is putting on a show. The Shepherd is putting on a show. He is putting us on display in a good way. He is featuring us here and now as His sheep, right here where we live. God is saying to this world, "Look at my sheep. Look at what I have created and what I have done in my sheep." We represent the shepherd. The condition of the sheep indicates the kind of shepherd they have. If they are looking poor, their wool is torn, they are dirty, they are hungry and restless, that indicates the shepherd is no good. We have a Shepherd that has invested in us and prepared us, to put us on stage before the whole world, not only to men, but even to angels. He has put us on display.

This will be done in an even greater way when we arrive in the Father's House. In Ephesians 3:20&21, we find that God is going to display the riches He has in His Christ through the church, world without end. When God gets us there and puts us in the eternal fold, He is going to put us on display for the angels. He will say, "Look, angels, you have been wanting to see it, my church. Here it is. Take a good look." Peter mentions this in I Peter 1:12. Our Good Shepherd features his sheep.

Do you really represent your Shepherd when He puts you on display? In the Roman theater sometimes you could see drama, both comedy and tragedy. It is like us going to the theater. They would take one of those comedies or a tragedy and get people to act out the characters. If one of the actors was careless about his performance, they booed and threw him off the stage.

If he did not act his part well, it reflected on the director. After they booed him off the stage, they would not let him back on stage. Do you represent your Shepherd, or are people getting the wrong picture from your actions?

Paul says in II Corinthians 3:2&3, "Ye are our epistle written in our hearts, known and read of all men. Forasmuch as ye are manifestly declared to be the epistle of Christ ministered by us, written not with ink, but with the Spirit of the living God; not in tables of stone, but in fleshy tables of the heart." An epistle of Christ means we have the message of Jesus in us. Other people may know Him by what they see of Him in us.

There are four Gospels printed in the Bible, but there is a fifth gospel as well. Matthew, Mark, Luke and John are not the only gospels. There is another. People are not reading Matthew, not reading Mark, not reading Luke, not reading John; they are reading the fifth gospel, the gospel according to you. They read it in your daily life.

I guarantee you that your neighbors are reading it. Are you a good representative of your Savior, your Shepherd? Do you display Him through you the way He means for you to? Every sheep when it's in its maturity, when it's well cared for by a good shepherd, speaks out, "I have a good shepherd doing right by me. I am properly representing my shepherd. The shepherd features his sheep."

Chapter Eight

THE SHEPHERD'S RELATIONSHIP WITH THE SHEEP (continued)

I.

I. THE SHEPHERD FELLOWSHIPS WITH THE SHEEP

The shepherd will take a sheep into his bosom, play with it, place it on the ground and it will gambol around in joy. The sheep enjoy the fellowship of the shepherd. Nothing gives the shepherd more joy than his time of fellowship with his sheep. John writes for us, concerning the sheep of God's pasture in I John 1:7, "But if we walk in the light, as he is in the light, we have fellowship one with another, and the blood of Jesus Christ his son cleanseth us from all sin." Also in I John 1:3, "That which we have seen and heard declare we unto you, that ye also may have fellowship with us: and truly our fellowship is with the Father, and with his Son Jesus Christ."

II. THE SHEPHERD FLEECES THE SHEEP

Psalm 95:7 says, " . . . we are the people of his pasture, and the sheep of his hand . . ." Again, in Psalm 100:3, we are called "the sheep of His pasture." Sheep need to be fleeced for several reasons. First, a sheep will not grow a new crop of wool if it is not sheared. Second, the wool will waste. Third, the wool must be removed for the health of the sheep.

This also applies to the sheep of God's pasture. The prophet Haggai writes in Haggai 1:6, "Ye have sown much, and bring in little; ye eat, but ye have not enough; ye drink, but ye are not filled with drink; ye clothe you, but there is none warm; and he that earneth wages earneth wages to put it into a bag with holes." The apostle James said in James 2:5, " . . . Hath not God chosen the poor of this world rich in faith, and heirs of the kingdom which he hath promised to them that love him?" And again in James 4:3, "Ye ask, and receive not, because ye ask amiss, that ye may consume it upon your lusts." We should understand from these truths that excess wool is not good for our spiritual health.

III. THE SHEPHERD FLAILS THE SHEEP

That means he uses his rod on them. He uses his strength on them. He uses his staff on them when they do wrong. The Bible talks about sheep going under the rod. That means under the chastening and control of the shepherd. He puts the rod on their back and he controls them with it. He is the one who does it all the time. He constantly keeps his sheep under control. If they do wrong, he corrects them and gets them back under control. He will not allow a sheep to stay out of control. He has his methods to achieve his purposes. Sometimes he may need to cross a stream of water. He will not lead his sheep the long way around it because some of them may get fatigued. But when the water is drifting, noisy and forceful, sheep will not go in it.

That is why the psalmist talked about the quiet still waters. Sheep will not even drink water that is rippling and running. They have to have water that is clear. They want to be able to see in that water. They do not want to drink if there are snakes or any other beasts in it. They want to see themselves in the water. The sheep will not cross if they cannot see any possible dangers. So the shepherd will find a lamb and cross with it in his arms. He will pull the wool and make it bleat. The mother ewe will look up, see it across the water, and will come after it. When she goes in that water the rest of the flock will follow her, and you know sheep follow one another.

Have we not seen and heard of our Great and Good Shepherd reaching down to pull a sheep from his pasture in order to get its parents attention? That is a natural love, not hate. The Good Shepherd has not chastened his sheep out of hate or anger even once. He loves them. "For whom the Lord loveth he chasteneth, and scourgeth every son whom he receiveth" (Hebrews 12:6).

The Great Shepherd does not correct from hate but out of love. When

God corrects, He is showing His love for the sheep of His pasture. Sometimes sheep are stubborn and unruly. A sheep's disposition most of the time is to be willing and yielding. But occasionally they get stubborn. If an old stubborn sheep will not stay in line and goes astray all the time, it will lead other sheep astray, because sheep like to follow each other. Sometimes the shepherd will turn to severe methods. He will take his rod with the knob on it, and he will break the leg of that old stubborn sheep. He then binds it up, takes it, lays it on his shoulder and carries it until it heals. That sheep becomes the leader of the file; it stays right close to the shepherd, and leads the rest of them. Veteran shepherds say after you break a sheep's leg it will never go astray again.

The Bible also talks about slaughter sheep. That means the shepherd will even take a sheep that is habitually stubborn and willful and actually set it aside for slaughtering. (Jeremiah 12:3) He will take its life. I John 5:16 says, "There is a sin unto death . . . "

God may allow the life of a man, one of the sheep of His pasture, to be cut off, because he will not obey Him. If an old willful, stubborn sheep of His just keeps going astray and will not be corrected by His chastening, God withdraws His hand of protection. He will not allow that sheep to stay out of control. It is an embarrassment to His holiness. Chastening is an expression of love. Punishment (or judgment) is an expression of wrath and God uses both of them. Chastening is not an expression of wrath; it is an expression of love. I know that a Christian cannot live in rebellion.

Paul tells us in Hebrews 12:8, "But if ye be without chastisement, whereof all are partakers, then are ye bastards, and not sons." The shepherd flails the sheep, out of love for them.

IV. THE SHEPHERD FOLDS THE SHEEP

Jesus said in John 10:9, "I am the door; by me if any man enter in, he shall be saved, and go in and out, and find pasture." Going to the fold does not refer to the statement at the end of the 23rd Psalm. "I shall dwell in the house of the Lord forever." The fold was used every day. But it is a typical truth about that eternal home. Day by day the sheep got an experience of going home to rest. The shepherd would take his sheep out every morning from the fold. He would get outside at the door, and stand there in the opening. It is an entrance without a material door. The shepherd became the door, and closed it off. He would get just at the edge of the door and call his sheep, name by name, and he would call them in order.

The one who came first stayed close to him, then they all came. They all lined up behind him and then he would take them out. He would take them to the grass in early morning, usually before sunup, while it was cool, and the dew was still on the grass. At that hour the sheep graze better and they do not get hot. The shepherd will graze his sheep until they are full and satisfied. Then, as they began to get hot, he would find a shaded nook somewhere by the still water, and they drank and lay down in as much shade as you could find in the Holy Land. They began chewing their cud.

A sheep has what is called rumen. It has two stomachs but the rumen is not like its regular stomach. A cow has two stomachs. Anything that chews its cud has two stomachs, but in sheep one is the rumen. When it bites grass off in early morning, it does not cure. The sheep just picks it off and swallows it. Sometimes the grass does not taste good. Sometimes it's dry and dusty. It has been in the heat and the dust.

When the sheep swallows the grass, it goes right to the rumen. Then the sheep will lie down. Then it will regurgitate it. The sheep brings that grass up out of that rumen, back into its mouth and starts chewing.

Here is what happened while it has been in the rumen. The grass has become the sweetest thing the sheep ever tasted. It has been in contact with the finest juices in that rumen; it's just so good tasting that the sheep do not like to swallow it, so they just chew it and chew it and chew it. That recalls what the psalmist says in Psalm 119. "Thy word have I hid in my heart," but then further down he says it shall be " . . . sweeter than honey to my mouth." Our equivalent of the rumen is our heart. Have you studied the word of God when sometimes it's dry, dusty and you cannot get anything from it? You could say that it is the driest thing you ever read. But as you kept on reading, putting it in the rumen, chewing it over in your heart, that is when it began to be sweet. The shepherd out there in the shade loves to see his sheep ruminate. Rumination to them is meditation to us. As you meditate you are ruminating, and God's Word is becoming sweet. We cannot bite off a little nibble of God's Word and run off and forget about it. We have to meditate. Sheep will do that in the heat of the day until the sun slants again.

Then the shepherd gets the sheep up, leads them to the grass and lets them graze and get full. Then he takes them to the fold, that stone enclosure. It has an entrance without fixed doors in the opening. The shepherd comes to that fold first, and steps right into the opening. Puts himself in the entrance and calls each sheep by name. He puts his rod down so that a sheep cannot enter, stops it. If it is too dark he takes his light and looks him over. He thoroughly examines the sheep to see if there's anything wrong. When his exam is completed, then he lets each sheep in.

When the sheep is not well, he takes his rod and pushes that one to one side and makes it wait. He puts them all in, even if he has a hundred in the fold. When he finds one missing, he will get the porter to take over the watch, and he gets his light and he heads out to find the lost sheep.

In a flock of one hundred, there might be four, five or six sheep that need his attention. He will take a light and thoroughly examine each of them. They may need some kind of oil, or I understand sometimes when they are cold and anemic he will give them wine mixed with water, which stimulates, or makes them warm. Some shepherds say it is cute when you find a little cold wet lamb, shivering, and you give it water mixed with wine. It is cute watching it wiggle its tail, which it does when it gets warmed up. The shepherd doctors them, treats them, puts them all in.

The shepherd will have them all in, including the strays. That is a typical day's journey.

There will come a day for us to be put in the eternal fold. The Great Shepherd will get all of his sheep in. Not one is going to miss it. We are headed for the eternal fold (Jesus called it "my Father's house") under the leadership of the Great Shepherd, and of all the sheep His Father gave Him, He has never lost, nor will He ever l one. John said in I John 3:2, " . . . it doth not yet appear what we shall be: but we know that, when he shall appear, we shall be like him; for we shall see him as he is."

Curtiss F. Lee, TH. B., TH. D.

Chapter Nine

The Nature and Habits of the Sheep

"He Maketh Me"

The Lord is my shepherd, I shall not want. He maketh me to lie down in green pastures . . . (Psalm23:1-2)

Make a joyful noise unto the Lord, all ye lands. Serve the Lord with gladness: come before his presence with singing. Know ye that the Lord he is God: It is he that hath made us, and not we ourselves. We are his people, and the sheep of his pasture. Enter into his gates with thanksgiving, and into his courts with praise: be thankful unto him, and bless his name. For the Lord is good; his mercy is everlasting; and his truth endureth to all generations. (Psalm 100)

Notice verse 3 says, "We are his people and the sheep of his pasture." John 10:4-5 says, "And when he putteth forth his own sheep, he goeth before them, and the sheep follow him: for they know his voice.

And a stranger will they not follow, but will flee from him: for they know not the voice of strangers."

John, 10:9-14: "I am the door: By me if any man enter in, he shall be saved, and shall go in and out, and find pasture.

The thief cometh not, but for to steal, and to kill, and to destroy: I am come that they might have life, and that they might have it more abundantly. I am the good shepherd: The good shepherd giveth his life for the sheep.

But he that is an hireling, and not the shepherd, whose own the sheep are not, seeth the wolf coming, and leaveth the sheep, and fleeth: And the wolf catcheth them, and scattereth the sheep.

The hireling fleeth, because he is an hireling, and careth not for the sheep. I am the good shepherd, and know my sheep, and am known of mine."

But ye believe not, because you are not of my sheep, as I said unto you. My sheep hear my voice, and I know them, and they follow me. (John 10:26-27)

I. THE NATURE AND HABITS OF THE SHEEP

The scriptures we have listed above concern the sheep, primarily. In this chapter I want to deal with what I call the natures and habits of the sheep. We need to know about them in order to understand them. We need to understand the comparisons God makes between His people and sheep so we will understand what He is teaching us.

Sheep are very peculiar animals. There are no animals on earth just like them. They are entirely different. They have a peculiar nature. They have a peculiar spirit. They have peculiar habits only found in sheep. No other animal is like them in that sense. In the Bible, there is not just one reference, but many, where God compares His people to sheep or sheep to His people, such as Psalm 100:3, where it says, "we are his people and the sheep of his pasture."

There is actually a grand likeness between sheep and people. Their glands are more alike than any other animals. So it is a kindly and good comparison God makes in the Bible, about the sheep and his people being alike. To understand this is to understand the sheep. I want to point out some of the marks of the nature of sheep. Remember, "HE MAKETH ME."

II. SHEEP ARE DUMB

They only know a few things. It is hard to teach them a lot of things.

They just do not understand; they are dumb. We never see a sheep that a shepherd has taught to do a lot of things. You can take a hog and make him jump through hoops in a circus. But you never see a sheep trained to do anything in a circus. They are dumb. They do not have much wisdom of their own.

They have to depend on another source for their wisdom. They just are not an intelligent sort of animal. They know the shepherd, and they know his voice, and they know how to follow him, but that is about the end of their knowledge. They are very limited in their knowledge. They know their shepherd well, but they do not know much else. They are dumb.

The Bible says that God does not call many wise (I Corinthians 1:26). What this means is that our knowledge of spiritual things on our own is very limited. We are very limited when it comes to heavenly worship. We are very much like the sheep at that point. Left to himself, man is ignorant about the things of God. A sheep knows a few things, but he is not a very intelligent animal. Dogs are wiser than sheep. A shepherd is wiser than a sheep. Lions, and leopards are lots wiser than a sheep. They are cunning and wise, but sheep are not very wise animals. We are pretty much like sheep when it comes to real wisdom. Remember, HE "MAKETH ME."

III. SHEEP ARE DEFENSELESS

There is nothing in their nature to defend themselves with. They just cannot defend themselves. They do not even hear well. If they get far off from the shepherd, they cannot even hear his voice.

Sheep do not see well, either. They cannot see at a long distance. Their eyes are never strong. They are not an animal with keen eyes and keen perception. They cannot run very long at a time without becoming exhausted. They become winded and lie down, and let whatever wild animal or whatever destruction comes, come on. They are just completely defenseless creatures. They have nothing to fight with. They are weak in battle and conflict. They are overcome readily.

The Bible tells us that we have no strength of our own. Paul says that our sufficiency is not of ourselves, but of God (II Corinthians 3:5). We are a lot like sheep when it comes to sufficiency. We are mighty weak when we are on our own. Paul says, " . . . when I am weak, then am I strong" (II

Corinthians 12:10).

Paul did not depend on his own power; he knew he was weak. He was a weak creature, except when he depended on the power of the Lord; then he was strong. Left to ourselves, we are weak, like the sheep, and therefore defenseless.

IV. SHEEP HAVE NO SENSE OF DIRECTION

This marks a sheep, very definitely. When a sheep starts going astray, it does not even sense that it's going astray. It goes astray unconsciously. It just gets away from the shepherd, gets lost and does not know which way to find itself, or what happened. It cannot find the shepherd. It has no sense of direction. It is the most helpless of animals when it comes to direction. The sheep may think, I sure would like to get back to the shepherd, but it does not know how. It is helpless and hopeless in its separation from the shepherd. It becomes more and more lost, more confused, more distressed and finally gives up, and just quits. Gets entangled, actually would die there if the shepherd did not come and get it.

When a sheep is left to itself, it certainly will always go astray, go farther and farther away from the shepherd, the sheep, the fold, and the flock. The Bible says that we are like sheep. "My people are prone to backsliding" (Hosea 11:7). We really have to rely on the power of God, the grace of God, and stay close to the Shepherd, or we will find ourselves drawn away. Paul said when he would do good, evil was present with him. It is out there all the time. We have a proneness to backsliding. We are that much like sheep. "All we like sheep have gone astray . . ." (Isaiah.53:6). The sheep goes astray heedlessly. It has no sense of going astray at first, and that is how we drift off. We Christians do not always willfully leave the Shepherd, we just sort of drift away. "I have gone astray like a lost sheep; seek thy servant . . . " (Psalm 119:176).

"I am not going to have any more to do with Jesus." I never knew a real Christian to ever make up his mind like that, did you? But they do get away from Him. They have a proneness to do it, and all without consciousness of it. We can get in a stream, and sit down in a boat with no oars, and then we go downstream. Sheep are like that. They are made up like that. We are, too. We have the backsliding tendency in us to drift away. We have to exercise the will to do right. We have to exercise our God-given will to stay in the presence of the Shepherd.

V. SHEEP ARE EASILY DISTURBED

Sheep will scatter in a minute. You can get them frightened so easily. A sheep is a fearful sort of animal unless is has a shepherd always in sight.

We are so like sheep. You can disturb sheep, you can frighten them, you can just scare them to death and they will get scattered. That is why the shepherd is so careful about leading them out early in the morning to the grass. We need to graze on God's Word early each morning, to avoid becoming disturbed about the things we will encounter each day.

VI. SHEEP ARE WEAK

When the shepherd takes the sheep to the grass, if the journey is long, just before he gets to the grass, he will make the sheep lie down and rest. Sheep tire easily and will not even graze if they're weary. They may graze a little bit, but they just do not have the strength. They are not strong animals. They are weak creatures. We all think we are somebody strong, but most little things will knock us over and knock us off track. We do not have much strength. We sheep must depend on the Lord; we do not have any strength of our own.

Romans 5:6 says that " . . . when we were yet without strength," Christ died for us. That means we do not have any strength at all. Sheep are weak creatures and God said His people are that same way.

VII. SHEEP ARE GREGARIOUS

They like to flock together. They follow one another. Let one sheep jump through a fence and every one of them will go with him. Let one cross a bridge, the rest will follow him. They stay together. They play better together than separately. It is essential they stay together. If one sheep goes astray, it will get in trouble.

A Christian does not do very well on his own either. We need the fellowship of other Christians. That is the way the body of Christ is prepared. Every part is essential. Every member of Jesus' body (the church) is absolutely essential to every other member of the body (Ephesians

1:22&23). We have to have each other in this body. Each member of this body supplies the other. We depend upon each other. Hebrews 10:24 tells us, " . . . consider one another to provoke unto love and good works." It says we need each other's daily fellowship. Let one get alone and the beasts of the wild will gobble it up. A sheep has no chance by itself. We need everybody we can get on our side, too.

VIII. SHEEP ARE AFFECTIONATE

They love their shepherd, they love each other, and they love to be loved. They like their shepherd to take them in his arms and fondle them. They like him to play with them. They will frolic around the shepherd, wiggle their little old tails, and just have the greatest time. They are affectionate animals. They have to have affection. Sometimes during the day while the shepherd is leading them, he will stop, and some old sheep will step out of line and look up and say, "baa." The shepherd will put out his hand and say, "Come.' Call out its name and say, "Come.' The shepherd may rub it on the head, or on the chin, give it a stroke on its back, and speak lovingly in its ear. "Do you like your shepherd? Has he been good today? Did he treat you well?" Sheep like it. They are affectionate animals. They are loving.

I do not know any subject with more emphasis in the Bible than "love one another." We are told 21 times in the Bible to love one another. That is in the New Testament alone. Jesus said, "A new commandment I give unto you, that ye love one another; as I have loved you, that ye also love one another" (John 13:34). That is the new commandment. Man is to be an affectionate animal just as sheep are

IX. SHEEP ARE CLEAN-NATURED ANIMALS

Sheep do not like filth. You cannot get a sheep to lie down in hog water to save your life. He might fall in it but he will start bleating, and want somebody to get him out quick. They are clean-natured animals. They will not eat filthy food. The Word of God talks about us being clean, being sanctified, and being holy. You cannot look at filth without getting filthy. Sheep do not stay around or dwell with filth. They're clean-natured animals.

X. SHEEP ARE WILLING ANIMALS

They have an unusual willingness about them. They are the most willing animals you will ever see. They are willing to follow the shepherd. They just go after him. They are willing to give wool without ever resisting him. They will not bleat, or fight back. Sheep will let you cut the wool off and never once hate you for it. They are willing actually to die without resistance. As a lamb before the slaughter, Jesus was led (Isaiah 53:7). Sheep are willing creatures. Willing to go right into death for their shepherd. They have no hate or rebellion or resistance and hardness. A goat, on the other hand, will never lose his spirit of rebellion, stiff neck and hardness.

XI. THE SPIRIT OF THE SHEEP'S NATURE

Sheep are not only marked by natural traits, but by spiritual traits also.

1. Sheep have a spirit of Meekness. You have heard the expression, meek as a lamb. That is what we mean. Sheep are meek and mild animals. They are not offensive. They do not have a spirit of contention. We are told in the Word of God: that is to be the spirit of the saints of God. In Titus 3:2 Paul says, "To speak evil of no man, to be no brawlers, but gentle, shewing all meekness unto all men." Ephesians, Chapter 4 and many other places in the Bible say the same thing. We are to be a meek people - to have that kind of spirit about us, a spirit of meekness. Most of us want to be strong, stout, self-sufficient, and our life is so important. Everything but meekness marks a lot of us. We were made up like that, until the Spirit of the Lord found us. Remember, "HE MAKETH ME."

2. Sheep have a spirit of Gentleness. They are not wild; they are domesticated. They are not hard to control. They are broken type animals. Broken in spirit. You do not have to break them like a wild horse. A sheep has a spirit of gentleness about it. The Word of God calls upon us to be gentle like that. We are to have what James describes as wisdom in James 3:17. "But the wisdom which is from above is first pure, then peaceable, gentle, and easy to be intreated . . . " Remember, "HE LEADETH ME."

3. Sheep have a spirit of Peacefulness. They are peaceful animals. They are peaceable. They have no spirit of conflict or fighting. They just want to be peaceable. If they do not have peace, they become an upset and disturbed group of creatures. They never try to startle one another. They want to have a peaceableness among them. An old goat will upset the peaceableness. He will destroy it. He will upset the peacefulness everywhere. He will not allow peace to reign. He is a contender. He is a fighter. He is rebellious. He likes to tear up everything, and keep a ruckus or an uproar going. He likes to have a disturbance going on. He likes that, unlike sheep. Did you ever see an old goat get in the church, put them in an uproar? Get a ruckus started and tear the whole thing up? As a child of God you're not like that. Sheep have a spirit of peacefulness about them. Hebrews 12:14 instructs us, "Follow peace with all men . . ." Remember, "I WILL NOT FEAR."

4. Sheep have a spirit of Contentedness. They are easily satisfied. They will lie down and chew their cud for hours and hours in contentedness. They are contented animals. They lie down in the green pastures, for their good, and the shepherd sure likes to watch them in their contentedness. There is no evidence of restlessness in a sheep's spirit. I Timothy 6:6&8 says, "But godliness with contentment is great gain . . . And having food and raiment let us be therewith content." And Hebrews 13:5 says, "Let your conversation be without covetousness; and be content with such things as ye have . . . " That is what God says to the sheep of His pasture. Sheep always go with the shepherd. You do not hear them bleating and butting their heads and fighting him over his provisions. They are content with what the shepherd gives them. They all have a still quietness about them. The sheep do not like anything noisy. Maybe that is why he leads them beside still waters. They don't like the rippling noise of water. They are not boisterous animals. They do not fall out with each other. They are not stormy. They have a quiet attitude about them. We should all have that spirit of quietness. It is wonderful. Peter and Paul in their writings express the virtues of "a quiet and peaceable life" and "a meek and quiet spirit." Remember, "HE MAKETH ME LIE DOWN."

5. Sheep have a spirit of Consideration. They consider one another and they consider their shepherd. They are not trying to push. They are not trying to take advantage. They are not seeking advantage. They continue giving consideration to one another and to the shepherd. Three places in the book of Hebrews, Paul asks readers to consider. Hebrews 3:1 says, " . . . Consider the Apostle and High Priest of our profession, Christ Jesus." Hebrew 12:3 says, "For consider him that endured such contradiction of sinners against himself . . . " And Hebrews 10:24 says, "And let us consider one another to provoke unto love and to good works." If you're the right kind of sheep, you are not trying to take advantage. Have consideration for each other. That is the spirit of a sheep. Remember, "THOU PREPAREST A TABLE."

6. Sheep have a spirit of Dependence. Sheep are trustful animals. They trust their shepherd; they trust him with their life. When they are near him, he has them under his control. They do not question or doubt a thing. They have a spirit of dependence on him. The fact is they have to depend on him for so many things about their lives that the sheep have to trust the shepherd. They could not get grass, they could not get water, they could not get protection, they could not get to and from the fold. As a matter of fact they could not even get in the fold. They are totally dependent on the shepherd. They really rely on him. Day in and day out, moment by moment, the sheep are relying on their shepherd. They are totally trusting him. Remember, "MY CUP RUNNETH OVER."

7. Sheep have a spirit of Willingness. David writes to us concerning Jesus in Psalm 110:3, "Thy people shall be willing in the day of thy power . . . " Remember what Jesus said in John Chapter 10. "My sheep hear, my sheep follow, my sheep know. I give them eternal life. They shall never perish." Sheep were always following the shepherd. They knew that wherever he was, all their needs would be supplied. They also knew he would take them through the valley of the shadow to return to the fold. How could we not trust such a Shepherd? Remember, "I WILL DWELL IN THE HOUSE OF THE LORD FOR EVER."

Curtiss F. Lee, TH. B., TH. D.

Chapter Ten

THE PERILS OF THE SHEEP

"I Will Fear No Evil"

Yea, though I walk through the valley of the shadow of death, I will fear no evil: for thou art with me; thy rod and thy staff they comfort me. Thou preparest a table before me in the presence of mine enemies: thou anointest my head with oil; my cup runneth over. (Psalm 23:4&5)

Notice that verses 4 and 5 mention some perils - the valley of the shadow of death, evil and enemies. Hosea, 13:7& 8 says, "Therefore I will be unto them as a lion: as a leopard by the way will I observe them: I will meet them as a bear that is bereaved of her whelps, and will rend the caul of their heart, and there will I devour them like a lion: the wild beast shall tear them."

Notice the perils for the sheep in these verses - the lion, leopard, bear, and the wild beast. Acts 20:28-31: "Take heed therefore unto yourselves, and to all the flock, over the which the Holy Ghost hath made you overseers, to feed the church of God, which he hath purchased with his own blood.

For I know this, that after my departing shall grievous wolves enter in among you, not sparing the flock.

Also, of your own selves shall men arise, speaking perverse things, to draw away disciples after them.

Therefore watch, and remember, that by the space of three years I ceased not to warn every one night and day with tears." Notice the perils in these verses - grievous wolves, and false shepherds.

The sheep will walk through the valley of the shadow of death and fear no evil for thou art with them. Thy rod and thy staff they comfort them. Thou preparest a table for them in the presence of their enemies.

There was no way in the days gone by in the Holy Land for a shepherd to care for his sheep without them facing dangers and perils. They always had them; they were always there.

When you get saved, you may get more problems and more enemies then you have ever had in your life. We get all the friends of Jesus when we accept Him as Lord of our life, but we get all His enemies too. When you take Jesus, you will line up against every enemy of Jesus. You will have some perils when you become a Christian in this world.

This world is absolutely against Christianity. Jesus said, " . . . In the world ye shall have tribulation . . . " (John 16:33). There were perils from the time the shepherd took his sheep out of the fold in the morning, as he stayed with them all day, and when he brought them back into the fold at night to bed them down. They were in great danger every step of the way. To some extent they were in danger in the fold. Sometimes, a thief would bound over the fold, sometimes thieves and robbers would slip in. The scripture says they climbed up some other way as thieves and robbers. That's what they do.

So there are perils confronting the sheep, and so it is with God's people. You cannot live in this world without facing dangers and perils. Let me classify these perils.

I. THE PERIL OF ENERVATING

Sheep could become easily enervated; lose their strength. There were things that would cause them to become distracted while walking on their journey. They had to go through very diabolical places. We mentioned the valley of the shadow of death. That is a hard climb. The actual valley of the shadow of death is very diabolical to get through. Their life is hard. Most of the terrain is hills, mountains and valleys, with rock ledges and gorges of all kinds. Living there when the sun gets up, they get awful hot. Sheep can easily become exhausted in that kind of conditions. That is why their shepherd is so careful about his sheep. Out there they could get sunstroke, and would be done for. They would lose the strength to go any further. They would be in serious trouble with sunstroke.

The sheep also get enervated from disease. They may pick a poison weed. The sheep are subject to scab disease. It was so concealed under the wool, unless the shepherd, as I wrote before, took his rod to separate the wool, to find it, or notice it. The sheep would lose strength and, the first thing you know, the sheep would be doing poorly, its wool would fall out, and it might not recover. That is why the shepherd always looked for the scab. That is where the saying comes from, "You cannot pull the wool over his eyes." The shepherd parted the wool, and you did not hide that scab from him, because it would absolutely enervate the sheep.

That scab represents sin in your life - secret sins you cover up and hide. They are under the wool. The wool is your thoughts and your convictions. You will get enervated. Sin will absolutely debilitate you and make you unable to stand as a Christian. We are not strong. None of us is so strong we cannot get enervated spiritually. So we are face-to-face with the fact of being the sheep of God's pasture.

II. THE PERILS OF THE ENVIRONMENT

In the Holy Land there are few parts of the environment that are good for sheep, without a good shepherd.

1. The elements. The day is extremely hot. There is extreme heat that will give you sunstroke. Humidity is always a hard thing. But out in the dry heat in that arid country you are more likely to get sunstroke. You have the extreme heat, then the cold night. There can be 100 degrees difference in temperature in 24 hours between day and night, and it is a very sudden change. There are storms coming down upon the Sea of Galilee. Sometimes storms come from the desert. A desert storm is the worst kind. The shepherd would suddenly head out to a big rock somewhere and get all of his sheep in the shelter of that rock if a storm came up. If you live with the elements about you like these, you need a Good Shepherd. You will have the storms to come, not just weather storms. If you are a sheep in God's pasture you will be threatened by the storms of immorality, greed, pride, and being forsaken by others. Living in the world we are living in, you will have those kinds of elements to contend with. This world is just

not kind to Christians. As soon as the bread and fish are gone, the people of this world will abandon you. The world has every distraction that can absolutely destroy your spirituality.

2.   The terrain of the land. People who have been in the Holy Land and also in Vietnam and Korea have told me that the terrains are much alike. The Holy Land is rugged. The mountains, the hills, the valleys, especially the place the local shepherds call the valley of the shadow of death, are rugged. The sheep travel through those gorges, down past the darkest spot where lions abide in caves, and there also are caves with robbers in them. The journey takes them through places of danger. They would not make it without a good shepherd.

III. THE PERILS OF ENTANGLEMENT

Sheep can get entangled. Over and over they get entangled. Paul said in Galatians 5:1," . . .and be not entangled again with the yoke of bondage." II Timothy 2:4 says, "No man that warreth entangleth himself with the affairs of this life; that he may please him who hath chosen him to be a soldier." God has chosen us for His army and we must keep from getting entangled. It is so easy to get entangled. Sometimes, many sheep will get entangled. A sheep will be going along with the flock, and will see a blade of grass, go after it and become entangled in a cactus or briers. Then it gets more entangled, when it tries to pull out. It cannot pull itself out and gets hung up by its wool. It will struggle and struggle until it is exhausted, and will be there until the shepherd comes after it.

The sheep of God's pasture get entangled in worldliness. People like to see the world. They decide that, well, they will copy it. They are acting like it and look like it. Sometimes they talk like the world as well. Some are dressed like the world, and want to imitate Hollywood. There's no time left for God in their lives. They cannot follow the shepherd when they are dragging all that baggage along. They become so materialistic, entangled in materialism.

Many Christians become entangled in all kinds of preoccupations. This world will keep you so preoccupied with so many things you will not have time for the right things. It will keep you busy, busy, busy, busy, busy - about nothing but your job and yourself. The world will keep you away from the main things. We live in grave danger of entanglement today. Some get entangled in religious programs. They are not able to read God's Word or look for God's sheep because they are so busy promoting their pet religious programs.

IV. THE PERIL OF ENEMIES

The sheep in the Holy Land had some potent enemies. They lived in the midst of them every day. There were wild and ferocious animals. They are not there now, but there was a time they were all there. In those days, there was danger.

1. The Lion. The lion was a deadly enemy of the sheep. Remember how David had to kill one (I Samuel 17:34&35). The lion devours you when he picks you. He will pull the limbs from the body and swallow them whole. He does not chew you up. He just swallows you whole. Takes you out, lies down and absorbs you. Takes seven days to do it, then he is hungry again, and he is dangerous then. The lion represents the devil. " . . . the devil, as a roaring lion, walketh about, seeking whom he may devour" (I Peter 5:8). You have him tracking you if you are keeping God's Word. The lion is shrewd about getting a prey. Watch a cat find a bug. It does not make any noise, just slips up on it. The cat comes from the lion family. That old lion stalks; he slips up on you. He watches his prey until the right time, and when he knows he has it, he springs. When he gets there, then he roars at the prey. The Bible says when the lion roars all the beasts lie down. They are scared of him. They want to hide. He puts fear in the hearts of all beasts. He scares them so much that he freezes them. They freeze in fear.

2. The Bear. This is what the bear does. The bear loves the flesh and the meat on your bones. It will not eat the bones. It will eat all the flesh off the bones and leave them. It likes the meat, the flesh. The bear represents the flesh. If you are a Christian, you are not perfect and the flesh can overcome you at any time, if you are not close to

the Shepherd. We live in great danger of the flesh every day. Paul said in Romans 7:18, "For I know that in me (that is, in my flesh) dwelleth no good thing."

3. The Leopard. The leopard is a cunning, smooth, wise, slick animal that knows how to get what it wants. It just cuts the throat of the sheep, sometimes to drink the blood. It watches them, keen in its observance of them. Unknown, unannounced, without anybody knowing how, it strikes. We are like sheep to the leopard, which is this world with its enticement to us. It is wise, it is shrewd, it is intelligent; it makes you accept what it has and carries you away. We have to be careful of this world every day we live in it. This physical world we live in is not our friend today. It will absolutely observe you, watch you, then entrap you, entangle you, strike you, and be gone. You can hardly cope with it. Paul said in Acts 20:3 and Acts 20:19 that those who were after him were lying in wait, which would be just what the leopard does.

4. The Wolf. In Matthew 7:15, Jesus told His followers, "Beware of false prophets, which come to you in sheep's clothing, but inwardly they are ravening wolves." Paul also warned in Acts, Chapter 20 about wolves that "enter in among you." They look like sheep; they will deceive you. They are experts at looking like they are one of us. Jesus also warned in Matthew, Chapter 24, that many are going to be deceived by false prophets in the last days. Will you be one of the few that does not get deceived? We better stay mighty close to our Shepherd and let Him use His rod on us, which is the Word, and His staff, which is the Holy Spirit, to keep us from being deceived. When grievous wolves enter in, they do not spare the flock. Wolves have done so much to kill the sheep. They tear them and hurt and scatter them.

5. The Viper. Vipers are very dangerous to the sheep. They have their holes in the ground. They blend in with the grass; they look like the grass. They get in the grass, dig their holes, and there they are. Any

time a sheep gets close to that hole, the viper strikes it in the face. The sheep will die almost instantly. Our vipers are the demons that we let into our lives. There is just one door into demonism, and that is disobedience. That is how Saul got into it. He disobeyed God. Paul, writing about the coming of the Lord in I Timothy 4:1, said, "Now the Spirit speaketh expressly, that in the latter times some shall depart from the faith, giving heed to seducing spirits, and doctrines of devils." He also mentioned in Ephesians 2:2, " . . . the spirit that now worketh in the children of disobedience."

6. The Robbers and Thieves. They are wicked men that go in groups of three to five, lie in secret and hide. They steal sheep that are lagging behind the shepherd. Wicked men are the enemies of God's children. Paul prayed to be delivered from unjust and wicked men. Wicked men like to bring you down to their level. They like to get you doing the same things they do. They not only do these things that are ungodly, but they take pleasure in doing them. They try to get you to do the same thing they are doing. They want to get you involved with unjust and wicked men. They will try to get you to just quit the way of righteousness. But if you have been born again into the fold of God, you cannot quit, because goodness and mercy shall follow you all the days of your life, and you will dwell in the house of the Lord forever.

Curtiss F. Lee, TH. B., TH. D.

Chapter Eleven

THE SHEEP'S RELATIONSHIP TO THE SHEPHERD

"He Leadeth Me"

The Lord is my shepherd. I shall not want. He maketh me to lie down in green pastures. He leadeth me beside the still waters. He restoreth my soul. He leadeth me in the paths of righteousness for his name's sake. Yea, though I walk through the valley of the shadow of death, I will fear no evil, for thou art with me. Thy rod and thy staff they comfort me. Thou preparest a table before me in the presence of mine enemies. Thou anointest my head with oil. My cup runneth over. Surely goodness and mercy shall follow me all the days of my life. And I will dwell in the house of the Lord for ever. (Psalm 23)

There are some scriptures in John, Chapter 10 that I want to call your attention to, that directly speak to the sheep's relationship with the shepherd. First, look at John 10:3-5: "To him the porter openeth; and the sheep hear his voice: And he calls his own sheep by name, and leadeth them out.

And when he putteth forth his own sheep, he goeth before them, and the sheep follow him: for they know his voice.

And a stranger will they not follow, but will flee from him: for they know not the voice of strangers."

John 10:27: "My sheep hear my voice, and I know them, and they follow me."

You will find the emphasis upon the sheep in their relationship to the shepherd in these scriptures. It is a wonderful relationship that the shepherd has to his sheep. We have dealt with that in a few sections in the previous chapters. But is also a blessed relationship that the sheep have to the shepherd. Of course it is because of his relationship to them that they have their relationship to the shepherd. If he were not their shepherd, they could have none of the relationships we are studying here. I want to deal with these and some scriptures elsewhere in the Bible, as to how the sheep relate to the shepherd.

I. THE SHEEP FAVOR THEIR SHEPHERD

Favor. The Scripture says they will not follow a stranger, but they will follow the shepherd. That indicates that they favor him; they have a preference for him. Certainly the sheep do that. Why do the sheep favor the shepherd? Why do they prefer him? There are four reasons I will list, even though there are many others.

1. Because of his Preference for them. He tells them. He prefers them before they ever preferred him. Jesus said, "And other sheep I have which are not of this fold: them also I must bring . . . " (John 10:16). He already knew about them. He already had them. They had been chosen for the flock and for the fold. He had picked them out. Then when they become the sheep of His fold, they too are preferred sheep. He picked them out and they are to be the ones that are known as His sheep. They preferred Him and favored Him because He preferred them, and favored them. Jesus said in John 15:16, "Ye have not chosen me, but I have chosen you . . ." He preferred us; it wasn't that we preferred Him. He had made His own choice of us as a Good Shepherd. The sheep prefer and favor Him because he preferred them.

2. Because of his Perfect love for them. The Scripture said we love Him because He first loved us. We did not love Him first. He showed His perfect love for us first, and His love begat our love. He planted that love in our hearts. He made us the sheep of His pasture in love, because He first loved us.

3. Because of his Provision. Sheep know who gives them their needs; from whose hands all their provisions come - pasture, water, shelter, etc. The sheep appreciate him and favor him because from his hand come all their provisions - every one of them. So they prefer him, because of the provisions and favor him for that reason.

4. Because of his Protection. The sheep find out that when they have a relationship with the shepherd, he takes care of them. He protects them against all their bitter enemies - those I mentioned in the last chapter. These are the reasons (no doubt there are others), why the sheep favor the shepherd.

II. HOW DO THE SHEEP FAVOR THEIR SHEPHERD?

It seems to me there are six ways that the sheep favor their shepherd.

1. They favor his person. They prefer his person. There are many scriptures that speak on this subject. For example, in Psalm 42:1&2, the psalmist said, "As the hart panteth after the water brooks, so panteth my soul after thee, O God. My soul thirsteth for God, for the living God . . . " The psalmist is expressing a desire for God's presence.

    He wants Him. He prefers His Person. There is also a statement in Psalm 73:25, "Whom have I in heaven but thee? and there is none upon earth that I desire beside thee." The sheep prefer and favor the person of their own shepherd. They always do. Jesus said, "All that came before me were thieves and robbers: but the sheep did not hear them" (John 10:8). They looked over some other shepherds. They favored the person of their own shepherd, and they would not follow another shepherd. Some people have tried to get them to do that. The following incident was passed on to me from Dr. Avery Rogers about his knowledge of the shepherds in the Holy Land.

    It is an eyewitness report concerning three Arab shepherds in

Palestine. Each came and brought his sheep to a watering place. The sheep all mixed up together while those Arab shepherds conversed with one another. Then one of the shepherds started walking back up the path, and gave a certain call. A hundred head of sheep just lifted their heads up and started following him. He did not look back to see if they did. He knew they would.

Then a little later, another one quit talking to the last one and started on his way, and made his peculiar call, and a hundred more sheep went after him. By this time, our witness was very interested. He said to his guide, "Ask the last shepherd if I can call them, and see if I can get them to follow me." The shepherd gave his consent. When the witness started walking off, he made a call. Instead of following him, the sheep ran to the shepherd. It scared them. They would not have anything to do with him. Sheep go to their own shepherd. They favor his person.

They prefer him above all others. That is what Jesus meant when He said in Luke 14:26, "If any man come to me, and hate not his father, and mother, and wife, and children, and brethren, and sisters, yea and his own life also, he cannot be my disciple." Jesus did not mean that we should actually hate those closest to us, but He was making the point that we should prefer the Good Shepherd above all others. If we are to be His disciples, He <u>must</u> have our favor at the expense of all others. If you have the Lord Jesus Christ in your heart, you prefer Him above all others or anything else in this world. That is the way sheep respond. They just will not flirt with strangers. When a sheep does not follow the shepherd, and will not respond to his voice, we know one of two things about that sheep: he is either sickly, or he does not belong to that shepherd. A sick sheep will listen to the voice of a stranger. He cannot distinguish well. He listens to every kind of voice.

He will follow anything that looks like a shepherd. People who do that are spiritually sick or they are not the sheep of Christ - one of the two. It matters to the sheep what shepherd they have. The shepherd's voice matters to the sheep, and if you are a true sheep of His pasture, it matters to you. The truth speaks; sheep hear the voice of their true shepherd. They prefer his person above all others. Jesus said that His sheep will follow Him. They want Him, for a true child of God has a thirst for God, a real desire for His Person.

2. They favor his presence by following him. They want to be with him. I am amazed at people that do not have the desire to see the Good Shepherd face to face, above all else, when they get to the Lord's House. Psalm 16:11 says, " . . . in thy presence is fulness of joy; at thy right hand there are pleasures for evermore."

    Psalm 63:8 says, "My soul followeth hard after thee . . ." That means seeking constantly to get in His presence, like the hound following after the deer. Friends want to be in the presence of those they love. We will make every effort to get there and we will drive hard to do it. We will overcome difficulties in getting there. We want to be in the presence of those we love and prefer, and we will make it there.

    David said in Psalm 51:11, "Cast me not away from thy presence . . . " The sheep just cannot stand not to be in the presence of the shepherd. They may unconsciously go astray. But as soon as they get conscious of the absence of the shepherd, they get restless and discouraged. They favor his presence. The sheep would rather be with the shepherd than anyplace in the world. We need to enjoy the presence of God. The psalmist said in Psalm 100:2, "Serve the lord with gladness: come before his presence with singing." The sheep prefer the presence of the shepherd. They love his presence. They will get in his presence. Psalm 140:13 says, " . . . the upright shall dwell in thy presence."

3. They favor his presence by listening to what he proclaims. The Good Shepherd said, "They hear my voice." Sheep love to hear the voice of their shepherd. Whatever he proclaims to them, it does not

matter. They like it. To a sheep, the voice of one shepherd is not just as good as the voice of another. They want the one they know. They respond to his voice and not to the voice of another.

The voice of Jesus to a true Christian is that way. "They hear my voice." That means they obey it. They heed it. They respond to His voice. And they get to doing what He says. The voice of Jesus matters to a true Christian. It is important to us. This is another evidence that you are a sheep of His pasture. You love the Word of God. You love what He says and you want to obey it. If you do not want to obey it, you do not have an affinity for Him.

The sheep show their favor for the shepherd by their love for the other sheep of his pasture. The sheep favor the Shepherd's people. They favor the other sheep they are going around with. They would rather be with the flock then be with anybody else. They do not like to get mixed with a bunch of goats and have to run with them. When the Shepherd starts home, and they hear His voice, they will not stay mixed with sheep of another shepherd. The Bible says this is the way we know whether we are born again or not. It shows in how you treat God's people, and what you think of them, for it says in the Word of God, "We know we have passed from death unto life, because we love the brethren . . . " (I John 3:14).

You prefer them, too. You favor His people. You like to be with them; you can have fellowship with them. You have the time for them. " . . . for what fellowship hath righteousness with unrighteousness? And what communion hath light with darkness? (II Corinthians 6:14)" That is why you love the other sheep of God's pasture.

4. The sheep show their favor for the shepherd by favoring his paths. Notice Psalm 23 says, "He leadeth me in the paths of righteousness for his name's sake (plural paths)." The sheep follow in those paths. They like to walk where the shepherd goes. They do not pick one of

their own choosing, or make their own paths. They go in the one where he leads. They follow: they choose his path. They favor his path.

5. The sheep show their favor for the shepherd by favoring his pasture. "He maketh me to lie down in green pastures." He who knows God hears the Word of God. Sheep prefer and favor the path of their shepherd. That is the relationship that the sheep has with the shepherd. He favors the shepherd. It is a glorious relationship.

6. The sheep Fellowship with the shepherd. They go with him everywhere. They hear his voice and follow him. They share with him, and they share from his hands. Often, only the sheep praise the shepherd's fellowship or companionship. Out there by himself, all the companionship he has sometimes is his sheep. The sheep are pleased with it, and with the shepherd. They love that fellowship with their shepherd. I John 1:7 says, "But if we walk in the light, as he is in the light, we have fellowship one with another . . . ". A sheep will leave out of a grazing line sometimes, following him. When he stops and turns around, it will come up there, and frolic around him, and rub against him. They like him to pick them up in his arms and lay them in his bosom. They just like that kind of fellowship.

I John 1:3 says, " . . . truly our fellowship is with the Father, and with his Son Jesus Christ." That is Whom our fellowship is with. People have such foreign ideas about fellowship. You have heard people say, "Let's go down to the church, have a social and have donuts and coffee." That is not fellowship. We are just kidding ourselves. "Let's have fellowship around a cup of coffee." Cannot have it around a cup of coffee, either. It does not respond to you. It is not alive. You have fellowship around Jesus. Our fellowship is with the Father and fellowship means we are sharing with Him. We are entering into what He is, and what He does. We have to fellowship with Him. The sheep do that with their shepherd.

Our fellowship is with the Son. That is a glorious one. There is nothing that will satisfy the sheep, like the presence and the fellowship with the shepherd. They are rested, they're peaceable, they're calm; they're satisfied when he is present with them. If you take him away, watch them get restless, watch them get discouraged, watch them get upset. Just as soon as the fellowship is taken away, they miss that fellowship.

III. THE SHEEP FURNISH THE SHEPHERD

The sheep furnish him with about all he ever has.

1. They furnish him with fellowship, as we have just written. They give him fellowship.

2. The sheep furnish him with fleece. Every bit of their fleece goes to him. When it has grown out, long and fluffy, he cuts it off; they give it to him. They furnish him with fleece. You will do that, too, if the Lord is your Shepherd. You will furnish Him, if you are a wise person. Remember, when the wise men came at His birth, they brought gold, frankincense and myrrh. Instantly God told Joseph to take the baby Jesus to Egypt. The giving of those wise men from the east signified the divinity of our Savior. Jesus was to live in Egypt, so that God could fulfill the prophecy that said he would call His son out of Egypt (Hosea 11:1). When you help send the message of our Shepherd Lord to anywhere in the world, you are furnishing the fleece. Fleece has a monetary value to the shepherd. He could take fleece, sell it in the market, and get money. The sheep gave the money to him. He did not have to take it. They did not just give ten percent; they gave all of it. We are stewards of everything God has given us.

3. They furnished him cloth and meat. The sheep died to give their shepherd clothing and meat. That is sacrificial. Jesus laid down His life for us, and we should lay down our lives for the Great Shepherd, when necessary. That is what the sheep did.

4. The sheep furnished him with fat. They found a use for it in that day. The Bible says the fat belongs to the Lord. They did not cook with

it; they offered it up to God.

5. The sheep finished him also with fluid, milk to drink. That is where he got his milk.

6. The sheep also furnished the shepherd with fruit. They brought more sheep into their shepherd's flock. I know that as individual believers we cannot give birth to any other creature, but God uses us as an instrument of witness and testimony. God needs sheep to spread the Gospel. We are to furnish Him with a witness.

IV. HOW DO THE SHEEP FURNISH THE SHEPHERD?

1. They furnish him Regularly. The shepherd lives off his flock every day. As Christians, sometimes we just give every once in a while to ease our conscience. But as good sheep, we should give regularly. The Bible teaches that we are not to pick out one time of year we might like to give a little something in the offering, and then go our way. The Word of God teaches us that upon the first day of the week, you lay it aside, and that is regularly. Every Sunday is the first day of the week. That makes 52 offerings.

2. The sheep furnish the shepherd Profitably. It is good for the sheep to do so. If it does not give wool, there will be no new crop. If it does not give wool, the old crop will waste, get pulled out on briers and thorns. It will be a wasted crop, and the sheep will become more prone to the scab disease. Giving the wool is for its own enrichment.

3. The sheep furnish the shepherd Willingly. You do not have to tie a sheep down to take its wool off. You do not have to have anybody hold it down. The Word of God tells us that Jesus, called the Lamb of God by John the Baptist, died for us willingly like a sheep (Isaiah 53:7, John 1:29). Sheep furnish the shepherd willingly. I do not think God ever clipped anything from an unwilling old goat. But sheep are always willing.

4. The sheep furnish the shepherd Sacrificially. They die to give him supply. Many times they will go to the slaughter. (Read about Steven, James, and others in the New Testament, also in *Fox's Book of Martyrs*). Many millions of the sheep of God's pasture have given their lives in sacrifice for the Shepherd.

5. The sheep follow the shepherd. They follow him, and a stranger they will not follow. How do sheep follow the shepherd?

    A. First of all, they follow Instinctively. They will not follow a stranger. Sheep are very stupid about everything, except whom they follow. They will follow nobody else but the shepherd. They will not follow anybody around, except the shepherd. They will not hear another's voice. Some goats, who think they are sheep, will listen to anyone's voice. They are trying to find something they do not have. A sheep follows Jesus, the Chief Shepherd, instinctively. They do not hunt for another voice. They are just going after Him. That is why I get so appalled at folks that are chasing after gifts. Sheep do not chase after gifts. (If it is a gift, you did not ask for it, or receive it by asking.) They follow the Shepherd. And that is instinctive. There is nothing better than Jesus, the giver. As long as you do not have anything better, I will stay with Him.

    B. The sheep follow the shepherd Continually. His words, "they follow me", are in the Greek tense that means continuous action, and they never cease to do it. That does not mean a sheep will not go astray occasionally. But it has an affinity for his shepherd and still wants to get back and to follow. Peter followed Him, denied Him, and then still followed Him, anyway. Sheep can get off the trail, but the minute they find out they are lost, they are already disturbed, and they want to get back to the fold. So they are still following him.

C.   The sheep follow Devotedly. Dr. Rogers said he watched sheep in the Holy Land many times going somewhere with the shepherd. They go down the road, walking briskly. Those little old sheep just go after the shepherd. They follow him devotedly. They give him all they have. They stay with him. Some would say they follow doggedly. In Psalm 63:8, the psalmist says, "My soul followeth hard after thee . . . "

D.   The sheep follow the shepherd Obediently. They willingly follow him. The shepherd does not have to drive, or beat them; they go after him willingly. They follow in the paths of righteousness. They follow him going through the valley of the shadow, when it is hard. They just keep on obeying him, following him faithfully.

E.   The sheep follow the shepherd Safely. "Yea, thou I walk through the valley of the shadow of death, I shall fear no evil." The safest place you can be in this world is in the will of God, the Word of Jesus Christ, obedient to Him. That is a safe place. Outside of that, you are on dangerous ground. They follow him safely. Every sheep is in danger if it gets away from the shepherd. Lions will get them, leopards, wolves, robbers, or this world and its pleasures. Our Great Shepherd is the only one who can get us to the Lord's House, through this maze of things in this wilderness world, and bring us to the fold safely. The sheep of the Great Shepherd's flock "shall never perish" (John 10:28).

F.   The sheep follow the shepherd Always. "All the days of my life" is how long they will follow. Sheep do not follow him part-time, then leave off following him sometimes. They follow him all day, all the time. They go all the way with him. From the time he steps out of the fold in the morning, goes through whatever the day may bring, until he comes back to the fold at night and puts them away safely. It makes no difference how long the shepherd stays out, or how long he keeps them out in the open, the sheep follow him all the days of their lives.

Chapter Twelve

OUR SHEPHERD LORD

The Lord is my shepherd. (Psalm 23:1a)

There are a multitude of references in the Bible to Jesus as a shepherd. Of course, He is Lord and He is therefore the Shepherd Lord. He has a threefold shepherd-hood. Psalm 22 presents him as the Good Shepherd; Psalm 23 as the Great Shepherd; Psalm 24 as the Chief Shepherd. There are many more references to Him as a shepherd. When the Holy Spirit spoke through David here in the first verse of this scripture about the Lord as my shepherd, He was speaking of the Lord Jesus Christ. That is the way I will consider him in this chapter, the Lord our Shepherd.

I want us to give consideration first of all to the name, Lord. "The Lord is my shepherd." That word, LORD, when it is spelled in capital letters in the Bible, always means Jehovah. Jehovah is called that kind of LORD. There is another word in the Bible for God as Lord and that is used when you call him Master. It is not like this one. Judas always spoke to Jesus as master or teacher. There is no record that he ever called Him Jehovah, LORD. The rest of the apostles did, but Judas did not. Therefore, he never submitted to his lordship in reality. He looked upon him only as a teacher, never as his Lord.

When it is spelled in capital letters in the Bible, L-O-R-D, all four letters capitalized, it means that it represents the word Jehovah. The word Jehovah, this word LORD, is found 6,823 times in the Old Testament alone. So it is the most important name for the Lord. The word Jehovah is derived from the Hebrew word Hadaa, which means to be, a being. That gives Him personality and He is a being that is life. He is called a living God, so He is a being.

This chapter relates to the Lord's personality. I am glad He has that personality. The word, shepherd, is another name for the Lord and that in the Hebrew is Rohi. It is spelled R-o-h-i, but it is pronounced like R-oo-ee. So David calls the Lord Jehovah-Rohi, my shepherd. Jehovah is the primary word for the Lord. It is the name the Jews reverenced and would not even pronounce. The primary meaning of this word Rohi, means to feed, to lead to pasture and to tend the sheep. The Good Shepherd told us to do that. "Tend my sheep." "Lead my sheep." "Feed my sheep." Feed the flock with which you are placed.

It also means a companion or friend. It represents the idea of intimacy in sharing lives and in sharing food; in sharing what you have. The word Rohi as companion is found in Judges 11:38. The word Rohi as friend is found in Exodus 33:11, where it carries the idea of Moses' intimate relationship with God - very close, like a companion, like a real friend. That is the meaning of this word, Rohi. It is in the name Jehovah-Rohi, which David used, that this intimate relationship finds it fulfillment. Whenever you join them together, this intimate relationship finds its highest expression in Jehovah-Rohi - my Lord, my shepherd. It is the most intimate, closest relationship possible. The shepherd is to his sheep as Jesus is to His people. Everything that a shepherd is, in a spiritual way, and way beyond that, is in this name. That is something about the meaning of the person we are considering here.

I. THE NATURE OF OUR SHEPHERD LORD

It is presented to us in the Scriptures. "The Lord is my shepherd." Practice calling him "the Lord, my shepherd"; the word "is", if you will notice in your Bible, is in italics because it does not appear in the original Hebrew Scriptures.

1. He is a Preeminent Shepherd Lord. That means He is above all others. This is a name for God as the Lord who is supreme, sovereign, absolute. That is what it means. He is a supreme, sovereign, and absolute being. There is no other like Him. There is no other God before Him. There is no one else like Him. He is

supreme and above all. He said to Moses, "I am that I am." This means that this Shepherd Lord is the unconditional, unlimited, sovereign, supreme, absolute God. That is who He is. He is the all-powerful, all-sovereign Lord.

This is the greatest teaching of the whole Word of God. He stands as sovereign, supreme Lord of all the universe, therefore He is not limited in any way. He is an absolute being, not limited, not conditional. He is sovereign Lord. He is God, and therefore He is Lord of the whole universe. That is the kind of person that David said was his shepherd - a preeminent Lord Shepherd. This is part of His chief shepherd-hood that Peter talks about, The Chief Shepherd. In days gone by when shepherds went out in groups, they had a chief shepherd that stayed at the fold. They took implicit direct command from him. They were under shepherds to him. They would listen to him. He was the chief one among them. Yet, Our Shepherd is not chief among anybody - He is above everybody. He stands as the supreme Lord of the universe.

2. Salvation. Our salvation rests upon accepting Him and acknowledging Him as Lord. Some will say, "Jesus was my Savior; I came to have him as Lord later on." It does not work that way. If you did not receive him as Lord, then you did not receive him as Savior. Romans 10:9 says, "That if thou shalt confess with thy mouth the Lord Jesus, and shalt believe in thine heart that God hath raised him from the dead, thou shalt be saved."

In the book of Acts, Jesus is called Lord 110 times. In Acts, Chapter 2 Peter used the word "Lord" seven times: once for Jesus' life, once for His death, once for His resurrection, once for His humanity, once for His divinity, once for His faithfulness, and once for His Lordship. Acts 2:47 says, " . . .And the Lord added to the church daily such as should be saved." In Acts, Chapter 11 the word "Lord" is used eight times; in Acts, Chapter 13 the word "Lord" is used 7 times. Jesus is only called "Savior" twice in the book of Acts, and then, only in reference to Israel. In Acts 5:31, he is called, " . . . a Prince and a Savior for to give repentance to Israel, and forgiveness of sins," and in Acts 13:23, " . . . raised unto Israel a Savior, Jesus." You would think that since Luke the physician, the author of Acts, is giving us a record of the ministry of the Church during the first century, we would notice the emphasis on the Lordship of Jesus Christ, our Shepherd. Jesus Himself said, when He was lamenting over Jerusalem, in Matthew 23:39, " . . . Ye shall not see me henceforth, till ye shall say, Blessed is he that cometh in the name of the Lord."

3. Jesus' ability to be Savior rests in His Lordship. His savior-hood rests upon His Lordship. It absolutely rests upon it. If He was not God and Lord before He became your Savior, then He is no Savior. He has always been God and Lord. He is Lord first and His savior-hood rests in His Lordship. If He is not your Lord, He cannot save you. To be Savior, He must therefore be Lord. Then He is a preeminent Lord Shepherd. Remember that the thief on the cross said to Jesus, " . . . Lord, remember me when thou comest into thy kingdom" (Luke 23:42).

Of course, no man can call Jesus Lord except by the Holy Spirit. That means he would have to be born again before the Lord acknowledged him. We must confess Him as Lord, and really that is what David is doing in Psalm 23. He is confessing Him as his Lord. He is confessing Him as Jehovah. He is an unlimited, absolute being, but God is much more than that. This recognizes His purity. When David called Him Lord, he was also recognizing His purity. At the cross we see Him as Lord of our lives and we acknowledge Him, submit to Him and obey Him. The sheep always do that. I do not mean that 100 percent of the time sheep are obedient. David translated it into his own life and said, Lord, Jehovah. He's my Rohi, my shepherd.

4. He is a Present Shepherd Lord. I have mentioned that the word "is"

does not appear in the original text, which means that the Lord is Jehovah, that He is ever present. When Moses said to God in Exodus, Chapter 3, "Who shall I say sent me?" God said, "Tell them, I Am that I Am sent you." He is an ever-present Lord Shepherd. He is present in the past, in the present, and in the future. He is present, that is all. I do not know how to tell you any other way than that. He always has been present and always will be present.

Jesus claimed this name also. In John 8:58, Jesus said, " . . . Before Abraham was, I am." In Deuteronomy 33:27, Moses says that "The eternal God is thy refuge . . ." That is what eternal means - not the past, not the future, but the present. God is the eternally present one, right now. He has not had something that is past in His life. He has not had a past like you and I have. He does not have a future like you and I have. He has an eternal presence.

The only time the word eternity is used in the Bible, it refers to God. Isaiah wrote in Isaiah 57:15 that God described Himself this way, "For thus saith the high and lofty One that inhabiteth eternity, whose name is Holy; I dwell in the high and holy place, with him also that is of a contrite and humble spirit . . ." The writers are describing Him as that, as our present Lord. He is not past; He is not future. He is right now. Ezekiel records, "The Lord is there." to give us a name for God's millennium city, in the last four words of his book.

Sometimes a shepherd is silent. Out with the sheep, he does not say a word. He is there meditating and silent. Maybe he is sitting on a rock, just watching them, silent. Sometimes it seems like he is not present, but he always is. His sheep know that. They do not have to hear or feel him in those times to know his presence. There is nothing as reassuring for the sheep as the shepherd's presence. It is the most reassuring thing they can have.

5. He is a Personal Shepherd Lord. Notice David said, "The Lord is my shepherd." I want you to check out Psalm 23 to research your own

personality. Look at how personal the shepherd is. Look at the personal pronouns David uses referring to the shepherd. The word "he" is used four times, the word "his" once, the word "thou", three times, the word "thy" twice - ten personal pronouns regarding the shepherd. They make him a person. Then look at the personal pronouns regarding the sheep. The word "my" is found four times, the word "me" is found seven times, the word "I" is found four times - a total of fifteen personal pronouns that refer to David himself.

Christianity is personal. Psalm 23 says that the shepherd has personality. He's a person. Jesus Christ is not an abstract being. Some folks think that Jesus is just a historical figure; that these doctrines are just abstract, historical facts. They don't look at Jesus Christ, as real person. Some people believe the church is just a building, not a community of believers.

Unity groups such as the Unitarians believe that everything is God. They make God an abstract, not a reality or personality. But the Bible makes Jesus a person. He is not an "it", not at all. So you have a personal Shepherd Lord and He relates to you as a person. That means He can help you as a person, and He does. Paul said of Jesus in Galatians 2:20, " . . . the Son of God, who loved me, and gave himself for me."

The shepherd did not just look at his sheep as a flock. He had every one of them individually named. He dealt with every one of them individually. He gathered each one of them every day. He called them by name, early in the morning, each one of them. He led them to the grass and the water. If they went astray, he personally went after them. If they needed doctoring some way, he did that for them. When he got back to the fold at night, he put them in personally, individually. He did not try to cut corners and just say, "Get in that door." He stood in the door. He acted like a door, turning like a hinge, letting one in at a time and holding it to check it in. He called them by name and got them in, one at a time.   Jesus wants a personal relationship with you. Someone will ask, "What does this business about shepherd and sheep have to do with me?" to which I always answer with this word from the Apostle Paul. I Corinthians 9:9&10 says, "For it is written in the law of Moses, Thou shalt not muzzle the mouth of the ox that treadeth out the corn. Doth God take care for oxen? Or saith he it altogether for our sakes? For our sakes, no doubt, this is written . . . "

So we are to understand that these writings in the Bible have application to us. You do not get lost in the crowd; Jesus can fellowship with you in a personal way. It does not matter how many folks are around. Whether anybody else has anything to do with Him or not, you can. It is a personal approach. Nobody has any right to meddle with that personal relationship you have with Jesus. Nobody. God deals with you personally. It doesn't matter what others may do. He will hold you accountable for yourself. We will only answer to Him for ourselves.

6. He is a Provident Shepherd Lord. "The lord is my shepherd; I shall not want." The word Lord here is just one word really - Jehovah (pronounced yeh-ho-vaw). Another name for the Lord, a compound name stressing one of His attributes, is Jehovah-Jireh, (pronounced yeh-ho-vaw-yir-he), which means "The Lord shall provide." The first time this compound name is used in the Bible is in Genesis, Chapter 22, when Abraham's son Isaac asked his father, "Where is the lamb for the burnt-offering?" Abraham answered, "God will provide himself a lamb". He used the name Jehovah-Jireh for God - Jehovah provides - and that is what Abraham had in mind. He saw God as his provider.

7. He is a provident shepherd Lord. The rest of the way in Psalm 23, He shows us everything else He provided. We see the shepherd's Lord here. Then we see all these provisions the rest of the way, all the way into the house of the Lord forever. These are provisions. He is a provident shepherd Lord. The Lord will provide, Abraham said to

Isaac. God will provide himself a lamb. In the New Testament, the Lamb was Himself, in the person of The Good Shepherd, Jesus Christ. Abraham said God would provide Himself a lamb, and He did.

A.   The Shepherd Lord provides Compassion. He is compassionate with us. The scripture says that Jesus looked upon the multitude as sheep that had no shepherd, and was moved with compassion. He had a compassionate love for the lost sheep of the house of Israel. So strong is Hs compassion that it will compel Him, even when they go astray, to go after them. He did not leave them alone because they went astray. He did not sit back with cold indifference and leave them alone. He went after them. He loved His own; loved them to the end. Just because they went wrong did not mean He ceased to love them. He had a strong compassion for them.

B.   The Shepherd Lord supplies the sheep with Companionship. The shepherd lived with his sheep day and night. Everywhere they were, he was. He had fellowship with them. He would take them in his arms. He would lay them in his bosom. He would carry them on his shoulder. He would talk to them like you talk to a person. He had companionship with them. Fact is, there was not anybody out there much, besides him and his sheep. He and his sheep had companionship. Our fellowship is with the Father and with His Son Jesus Christ. They provide our companionship.

C.   The shepherd Lord provides the sheep Commodities: water, pasture, guidance, rest, peace, the fold, everything. He had every commodity they needed and He provided for them.

In Romans 8:32, Paul said, "He that spared not his own Son, but delivered him up for us all, how shall he not with him also freely give us all things?" All the commodities we need for a Christian life we find in the shepherd.

D.   The shepherd Lord provides the sheep with Control. He controls everything. He even controls the life of the sheep. If it is lost, he finds it. If it strays, he goes after it, corrects it, brings it back, and puts it in the fold. The next day he may chastise it. He gives it correction. He furnishes the control. He does not leave the sheep to guide their own lot and run their own show. Could you imagine, even one time, the shepherd and his sheep in front of the fold, in the morning, and him saying, "Listen, I want you to vote today on where we are going. Everybody that wants to go right, lift up your right hind leg. Everybody that says go left, lift up your left hind leg." He did not do that. Who ever heard of a shepherd asking sheep to vote?

The only time the disciples voted, they got in trouble. They elected the wrong man. That is right, they elected the wrong man. After the resurrection, Jesus said to the disciples, in Acts 1:4&5, " . . .wait for the promise of the Father, which, saith he, ye have heard of me . . . ye shall be baptized with the Holy Ghost not many days hence." Instead, what did they do, but call a meeting, and voted in Matthias to replace Judas, while all the time Jesus was converting Paul for the replacement. The disciples did not wait on the promise of the Spirit, but rushed to judgment without the spirit of wisdom. The shepherd provides control. The sheep are committed to it. The sheep are willing. They do not mind being under his control. He has the authority.

E.   The shepherd Lord provides the sheep with Correction. A child of God, a sheep of God's pasture, has to have correction. We are neither sinless nor perfect. Our Shepherd Lord will take us to the watering hole (repentance) by His own means (and He has them), wash us and get us clean. The shepherd will not allow His sheep to remain unclean. He washes them. He furnishes whatever correction they need.

F.   The shepherd Lord provides the sheep with Comfort. "Thy rod and thy staff, they comfort me." Your presence comforts me. "Thou art with me, and thy rod and thy staff, they comfort me." Sheep are comfortable, not in the sense that they are lazy and idle, but that they are calm and at peace. They are chewing their cud and satisfied. The shepherd knows when they're comfortable in that way.. They are producing flesh, fat, fleece, and fluid. They're getting along well. The shepherd Lord comforts them.

G.   The shepherd provides the Camp for the sheep. He provides the pen. He takes them to the fold and gets them in. That is the shepherd's loyalty that we have. David said in Psalm 23:6, " . . . I will dwell in the house of the Lord forever." Notice the assurance in "I will." Jesus told us in John 10:27&28, "My sheep hear my voice, and I know them, and they follow me: And I give unto them eternal life; and they shall never perish, neither shall any man pluck them out of my hand." That is assurance.

I have a sister who suffered her entire life. When she had just began to walk, she was kicked by a horse. After months of surgery, some of her brain was removed. She had normal intelligence, but it remained that of a child. She knew the Good Shepherd, by experience of the new birth, from the time she was a young girl. After suffering a long illness from breast cancer, she went to the Lord's House, at the age of 44. That is the reason I say I <u>have</u> a sister. But before she departed, she penned these words and gave them to me: "Thank you Lord, you helped me see. When you're in trouble, And in despair, Remember God is always there. His love is mighty, His love is true, For God has never forsaken you. And though you're down, And feeling blue, Remember

God! He still loves you. This is a story, but it's true, For God has suffered much more than you. He gave His son, to pay the price, that we might have everlasting life. For Christ died on Calvary, to bear these burdens for you and me. And I thank you Lord!!!! You helped me see, that you suffered much more than me." Norma Sheffield, May 16, 1986.

In the last chapter of our Bible we find these words concerning the Lord's House: "And he shewed me a pure river of water of life, clear as crystal, proceeding out of the throne of God and of the Lamb. . . And there shall be no more curse: but the throne of God and of the Lamb (OUR SHEPHERD LORD) shall be in it; And his servants (the sheep of God's pasture) shall serve him" (Revelation 22:1&3)

Curtiss F. Lee, TH. B., TH. D.

Chapter Thirteen

THE SHEPHERD'S PROVISIONS

"I Shall Not Want"

The Lord is my shepherd; I shall not want. He maketh me to lie down in green pastures; he leadeth me beside the still waters. He restoreth my soul; he leadeth me in the paths of righteousness for his name's sake. Yea, though I walk through the valley of the shadow of death, I will fear no evil; for thou art with me; thy rod and thy staff they comfort me. Thou preparest a table before me in the presence of mine enemies; thou anointest my head with oil; my cup runneth over. (Psalms 23:1-5)

Ezekiel 34:13-15,30&31. "And I will bring them out from the people, and gather them from the countries, and will bring them to their own land, and feed them upon the mountains of Israel by the rivers, and in all the inhabited places of the country.

I will feed them in a good pasture, and upon the high mountains of Israel shall their fold be: there shall they lie in a good fold, and in a fat pasture shall they feed upon the mountains of Israel.

I will feed my flock, and I will cause them to lie down, saith the Lord God.

Thus shall they know that I the Lord their God am with them, and that they, even the house of Israel, are my people, saith the Lord God.

And ye my flock, the flock of my pasture, are men, and I am your God, saith the Lord God."

In this chapter I want to list the many provisions the shepherd makes and supplies for the sheep.

These are the shepherd's provisions. We have the person of the shepherd stated in the first verse. "The Lord is my shepherd." Then there is a proclamation or declaration by the sheep. "I shall not want". Then follow the real provisions the shepherd makes for the sheep.

It is the duty and even the joy of the shepherd to provide everything his sheep need, desperately need. They have to be provided with certain things, or they will not survive. One is pasture. Another is water. Then of course there is guidance.

I. THE BASIS OF THE SHEPHERD'S PROVISIONS

First, they are based upon the nature of the person of the shepherd. David said, "The Lord is my shepherd." That means that Jehovah God is the Shepherd. In the statement, "I shall not want," is another expression of God as Jehovah-Jireh, which means provident Lord, because He is that kind of God, He is that kind of Shepherd. He provides for His sheep. He knows how to provide since He is the Lord, since He is Jehovah, since He is a provident God. He knows how to provide for them.

Not only that, but He is able to provide. The Lord, Abraham knew, provided the lamb, for the sacrifice in place of his son Isaac (Genesis 22:8,14). Nothing can keep Him from it, because He has a deep desire to provide for His sheep. He rejoices in providing for them.

The provisions are based upon the relation of the sheep to the shepherd. David said, "The Lord is my shepherd." Because of that relationship, the shepherd provides for his own. It is a relationship of love and concern, a matter of deep compassion for the sheep and a desire to see them well taken care of. Because they are his, he provides for them. The relationship necessitates the provision.

II. THE NATURE OF THE SHEPHERD'S PROVISIONS

1. They are All-inclusive. "I shall not want" means that everything a sheep needs, the shepherd provides. Whatever you need as a child of God, He provides in Christ Jesus. God freely gives us all things

(Romans 8:32). That is all-inclusive provision for us. Paul said in Ephesians 3:20 that God " . . . is able to do exceedingly abundantly above all that we could ask or think . . . " I can ask a whole lot, but I can think a lot more. Yet we cannot exhaust His supplies.

2. They are Adequate. There are no needs, at any point in your life, as a child of God, that cannot be met. His provisions are adequate for every kind of need that may arise, whatever the nature of it, no matter how severe.

3. They are Available. Notice that David said, "He maketh me to lie down in green pastures, and he leads me by the still waters." All these provisions are available to the sheep. If a sheep is hungry, he is led to green pasture. If he is exhausted, he can lie down there. If he is thirsty, still waters are nearby.

4. They are Applicable. The shepherd knows how to apply them to the needs of the sheep. Whenever the sheep has a need, the shepherd knows how to apply the provision for that need. He understands the sheep. The provisions are applicable to the needs of that sheep. The shepherd knows each sheep's taste and applies the provisions accordingly.

III. THEY ARE AMPLE

David said, "I shall not want." The shepherd picks out the provision that satisfies that want - whatever the want is in his life.

Not everybody who reads this Psalm can say in his heart, "I shall not want." because the Lord is not his shepherd. Remember the Good Shepherd, the Lord Jesus Christ, said, "My sheep hear my voice. I know them and they follow me." The Shepherd only supplies the sheep of His own flock. You must become a sheep of His pasture to be able to say, "I shall not want"

A few things have to take place in a person's life. I want to discuss those here. In order for the Lord Jesus Christ to fulfill His three offices of (Good, Great, Chief) Shepherd in a person's life, that person must be born of the Spirit. Jesus said in John 3:6, " . . . that which is born of the SPIRIT is spirit." He said in John 4:24, "God is a SPIRIT: and they that worship him must worship Him in SPIRIT and TRUTH." Romans 8:26 says, "Likewise the SPIRIT helpeth our infirmities . . . ". I John 5:12 says, "He that hath the Son hath life; and he that hath not the Son of God hath not life."

When a believer gets to this point, then he can say, "The Lord is my shepherd, I shall not want."

I shall not want for REST, because He maketh me lie down in green pastures. Acts 9:31: "Then had the churches REST throughout all Judea and Galilee and Samaria, and were edified; and walking in the fear of the Lord, and in the COMFORT of the HOLY GHOST, were multiplied." I Peter 4:14: "If ye be reproached for the name of Christ, happy are ye; for the SPIRIT of GLORY and of GOD RESTETH upon you . . ." Hebrews 4:9&10: "There remaineth therefore a REST to the people of God. For he that is entered into his REST, he also hath ceased from his own works, as God did from his." Galatians 5:5: "For we through the SPIRIT wait for the hope of righteousness by faith."

I shall not want for REFRESHMENT, because "he leadeth me beside the still waters." John 7:38&39: "He that believeth on me, as the scripture hath said, out of his belly shall flow rivers of living water. (But this spake he of the SPIRIT, which they that believe on him should receive: for the HOLY GHOST was not yet given; because that Jesus was not yet glorified.)" Titus 3:5: " . . . he saved us, by the washing of regeneration, and renewing of the HOLY GHOST."

I shall not want for HEALING, because "he restoreth my soul." Malachi 4:2: "But unto you that fear my name shall the SUN OF RIGHTEOUSNESS arise with HEALING in his wings . . . " I Thessalonians 5:23: "And the very God of peace sanctify you WHOLLY; and I pray God your WHOLE SPIRIT and SOUL and BODY be preserved blameless unto the coming of our Lord Jesus Christ." I Corinthians 6:11: " . . . but YE are WASHED, but ye are SANCTIFIED, but ye are JUSTIFIED in the name of the Lord Jesus, and by the SPIRIT of our God."

I shall not want for GUIDANCE because "he leadeth me in the paths of righteousness." Romans 8:14: "For as many are LED by the SPIRIT of GOD they are the sons of God." John 16:13: " . . . when he, the SPIRIT OF

TRUTH is come he will GUIDE you into all truth . . ."

I shall not want for COURAGE because "Yea, though I walk through the valley of the shadow of death, I will fear no evil, for thou art with me." Romans 8:15: "For ye have not received the SPIRIT of bondage again to FEAR; but ye have received the SPIRIT of adoption, whereby we cry Abba, Father."

I shall not want for COMFORT, because "thy rod and thy staff they comfort me." Notice it is "rod and staff, they" , not just one, but both. The written Word, our Bible (the Rod), and our Comforter (the Staff), which apply THE WORD, JESUS CHRIST (John 1:1), to our lives. John 14:16,17,26: "And I will pray the Father, and He shall give you another COMFORTER, that he may abide with you for ever. Even the SPIRIT of TRUTH; whom the world cannot receive . . . But the COMFORTER, which is the HOLY GHOST, whom the Father will send in my name; he shall teach you all things. . ."

I shall not want for NOURISHMENT, because "thou preparest a table before me in the presence of mine enemies." Ephesians 5:18: "And be not drunk with wine, wherein is excess; but be FILLED with the SPIRIT."

I shall not want for JOY in this life, because "thou anointest my head with oil; my cup runneth over. Surely; goodness and mercy shall follow me all the days of my life . . . " Romans 14:17: "For The Kingdom of God is not meat and drink; but righteousness, and peace, and JOY in the HOLY GHOST."

I shall not want for JOY in the life to come, because "I will dwell in the house of the Lord forever." Galatians 6:8: " . . . he that soweth to the SPIRIT shall of the SPIRIT reap life EVERLASTING."

I shall not want for ASSURANCE, because "The Lord is my shepherd. I will fear no evil: Surely goodness and mercy shall follow me. I will dwell in the house of the Lord forever." II Corinthians 1:22: "Who hath also SEALED us, and given the earnest of the SPIRIT in our hearts." Ephesians 1:13: "In whom ye also trusted, after that ye heard the WORD of TRUTH, the gospel of your salvation: in whom also after that ye believed, ye were SEALED with the holy SPIRIT of promise." Ephesians 4:30: "And grieve not the holy SPIRIT of GOD, whereby ye are SEALED unto the day of redemption."

I shall not want for COMPANY or COMPANIONSHIP because "thou art with me." Philippians 2:1: " . . . fellowship of the SPIRIT . . ." I John 3:24: " . . . And hereby we know that he abideth in us by the SPIRIT which he hath given us."

Truly, there is no end to His provisions. Whatever we need, God the Father has provided in the Lord Jesus Christ, and supplies them to us by the Spirit, from His Word. He provides us meekness, lowliness, goodness, Sonship, bread, light, door, Shepherd, resurrection, way, truth, life, true vine, and if there be any other thing we can even imagine, he has supplied it in Christ. Ephesians 1:3: "Who hath blessed us with all spiritual blessings in heavenly places in Christ . . ." Ephesians 2:6: "And hath raised us up together, and made us sit together in heavenly places in Christ Jesus." I heard one of God's teachers say, "Beside me are still waters, beneath me are green pastures, before me is a table prepared, between home and me is a valley, behind me are goodness and mercy, beyond is the Lord's House, all because the Lord is my shepherd."

Is He yours? The Lord Jesus Christ is called, THE GOOD SHEPHERD twice in the Bible. He is called THE GREAT SHEPHERD once; He is called THE CHIEF SHEPHERD once; He is called THE SHEPHERD AND BISHOP OF OUR SOULS once. He is called A SHEPHERD in Isaiah 40:11; He is called MY SHEPHERD in Psalm 23:1, but if he is not really MY SHEPHERD to me, all this amounts to nothing.

For the shepherd in the Holy Land, the two vital things he must provide for his sheep are the green pastures and the still waters. We will look at these in some detail in the rest of this chapter.

IV. THE SHEPHERD PROVIDES GREEN PASTURES

"He maketh me to lie down in green pastures."

Sheep are creatures that require grass. They must have grass for their food. They absolutely must have it every day. So it becomes the duty of the shepherd to provide the pasture.

In Ezekiel 34:14, God says, "I will feed them in a good pasture . . . and in a fat pasture shall they feed upon the mountains of Israel." It was the great joy and business of the shepherd to provide the green pastures for his sheep.

1. The performance of the shepherd. Notice what he said: "He maketh me to lie down in green pastures." The shepherd could not make him lie down in green pastures until he had provided the green pastures. He leadeth me to the green pasture and beside the still waters.

2. The pleasantness of the pasture. There are two things about it that make it a pleasant pasture. One is, it is green, the other is that the sheep can lie down in it. What does that mean - green pastures? The word green here refers to life. Remember when God said to Noah in Genesis, Chapter 9 that He would give a token of His covenant? We call it a rainbow. The bow in the cloud is a complete circle. We only see the bottom side of it and it looks like a bow. If you are on a plane, sometimes you see the whole bow. Around that complete circle is green. God is saying by the green, that life is going to go on; it will not be destroyed by a flood again. Life is continuous like the green around the rainbow.

V. THEY ARE LIFE-SUSTAINING PASTURES.

When the scripture says green pastures it is saying life-sustaining pastures. Green pastures are life-sustaining pastures. They have life in them. They are not dried up pastures. They have within them the ability to sustain life. Therefore, the shepherd is providing for the life of the sheep.

1. The color of the pastures shows life. Do you know why grass is green? It gets the direct sunlight. Its source of greenness is the sun. In other words, green grass means that green is the sun in the grass. If you take grass out of the sun, the sun will come out of the grass. It will turn white when it stays in a dark place. You have seen a run of white grass. You have seen Bermuda grass that has been under a dark place, maybe under a board, and you lift it up and that Bermuda grass is white. It hasn't any sun in it. The green is the sun in the grass. The Bible says that Jesus Christ is the Sun of righteousness

(Malachi 4:2). The thing that makes the Word alive is that the living Christ is in it.

2. There is symbolism in the green grass. What does green grass symbolize? It is not hard to find. It is the Word of God. If you want to know where green pastures are, they are the words on the pages of the Bible. Sometimes I say the Bible is a written Word and Jesus a living Word. Really the Bible is a living Word and Jesus is a presence of the Word. He is a presence. The reason the Bible is alive is because Christ is in it. When speaking of the Scriptures, Jesus said in John 5:39, "Search the scriptures; for in them you think you have eternal life: and they are they which testify of me." If you do not find Christ in His Word, you have not found the real life.

So the written Word testifies of Him we call the Living Word. He is the Living Word and the personal Word. Christ is the life of the Word, and this Word is alive because of Him. It is not just a dead book. A sheep has to feed on pasture every day. They tell us that only 12 percent of the Christians in America read their Bible daily; 88 percent do not. A large portion of that remaining 88 percent read it once a week, a little snatch on Sunday morning when they're going to go to Sunday school. They get their little Sunday school quarterly, get a little dab here and a little dab there, unconnected.

It's no wonder the sheep do so poorly. No wonder their wool is sorry. We need life-giving substance coming from the Word of God every day. We are not following the Shepherd if we do not seek to know His will every day. He makes us lie down in green pastures. Find out what God has for you. Have you ever read the Bible and let God speak to you through it? There is not a word in the Bible (when I speak of the Bible I am referring to what is commonly called the K. J. V., or the King James Version) that has not done something for me. I laugh at critics. It does not disturb me, when they try to tell me this is not inspired of God; that every word written is not inspired. It does not bother me. I know what God has said to me from it. God has already spoken to me from it. God has already fed me from it. I do not have to take somebody else's word for it. I've found I have the greatest theologian of all time in my life, since God saved me. The Holy Spirit is my teacher and He is yours. Since He is the author of the Word, is He not the only and best teacher of His own work?

We need to get back to God's Word. You will not make fat and flesh and fleece for your Shepherd if you do not feed on His green pasture. You will find out when you get through feeding that Psalm 23 is true. The place of the Word of God in the life of a Christian is surely emphasized strongly in this psalm. The Bible says God has magnified His Word above His name (Psalm 138:2).

3. The posture of the sheep in the green pasture. "He maketh me to lie down." First of all, it's a posture of repose. It is not a posture of idleness. This posture is very important to the sheep. In order for sheep to lie down, two things have to occur. First, the shepherd has to be present. With his presence there, the sheep will lie down. If the shepherd is not there, they will not lie down. It does not make any difference how green the grass is, the sheep will be scared and restless, if the shepherd is absent. The presence of the shepherd put the sheep in that state of repose. They feel safe to lie down then. They sought the presence of the shepherd, so they would not be afraid to lie down. His presence gave them that sense of repose.

   Second, to lie down requires the satisfaction of hunger. The sheep nipped the grass off all morning long. It gets too hot sometimes later in the day. The sheep have filled their rumen. It is tight. They knew when hunger was satisfied. A hungry sheep will never lie down. They are restless creatures without their hunger satisfied. You will be restless also, until you satisfy your soul with the Word of God.

4. The consequences of this repose. The sheep are not lying down to be lying down. That would be idle or lazy. There is a reason they lie

down. They lie down to chew their cud. They lie down to ruminate. I have mentioned before that the sheep has a rumen, a second stomach.

The rumen has all the necessary things to break grass down and turn the juices to sweetness. A sheep does not chew the grass it bites off. It does not taste good to its mouth. Sometimes it is dry. Sometimes it has a taste that's not good when the sheep bites it off and immediately swallows it. So the grass heads to the rumen. When it starts chewing his cud, it is ruminating. It brings the grass up out of that rumen while it is lying down. The sheep chews it as its cud. It does not like to swallow it, right away. To us, that is like meditation on God's Word. I do not mean just run in, bite some off and leave the rest. Psalm 119:97 says, "

O how I love thy law! it is my meditation all the day." If we are going to meditate, we have to fill our minds with His Word. Sheep cannot be grazing all the time and running everywhere. They have to ruminate, and we do, too. If we ruminate (meditate) on God's Word, we can say with the psalmist in Psalm 119:103, "How sweet are thy words unto my taste! yea, sweeter than honey to my mouth!" That's why the sheep lie down, to ruminate.

Your position of repose means, "I'm meditating on God's Word." There are certain consequences that come from meditating on the Word of God. You have a refreshed sheep. A sheep in a state of repose will get refreshed. When it makes its journey to the fold that night, it is refreshed. The food refreshes it, and the water refreshes it. The sheep is made strong. That grass strengthens it. The Word of God will make us strong, also. The shepherd knows while the sheep is lying out there chewing its cud, the fleece is growing, the flesh is getting firm, fat is coming on and it is making milk, fluid. You have a replenished sheep. The shepherd may take that milk at night or its lamb sucks it out; it is gone. The next day the sheep grazes, gets water, and ruminates and there is more milk; it is replenished. Well-fed sheep keep ruminating on the green grass, and get strong. They then go around with a good crop of wool, and are producing what the shepherd wants them to.

5. This posture of repose shows satisfaction. I just told you that a hungry sheep will not settle down. It is dissatisfied. It is restless and it will go astray. If it is not fed, it will go out hunting for pasture. I have seen some Christians like that, running here and there. They will try everybody's prescription. They will listen to all grand things that come along. Hungry people stray like sheep. A hungry sheep will not lie down and be calm. It will be a reckless creature. There is something necessary about the green pastures.

VI. THE STILL WATERS

"He leadeth me beside the still waters." Just as sheep must have the pasture, they cannot do without the water. They have to have both. Not just on certain occasions, but every day. Every day they have to have both. I want to point out the Spirit of the Shepherd, that I wrote about in chapter 3. "He leadeth me beside the still waters." He guides the sheep to the water. He does not leave them on their own to find it. He sees that they get there. His guidance is personal. Listen to what it says – both are involved. "<u>He</u> leadeth <u>me</u> beside the still waters." That is personal.

Sometimes the sheep will get in the water. It may be hard to find a place on the bank when all the sheep are there. They may have difficulty. There may be a little lamb running up and down trying to find a place. The shepherd will find an opening, and slip it in where it can get water. That is what David is talking about. The shepherd leads them right to it. He sees that they get water. He guides me, the Shepherd does, my personal way. His guidance is plain; it's clear, it's concise.

The shepherd takes the sheep to the water. It is not a confused thing. It is a very plain guidance to the water; it is a personal guidance. The shepherd does not aimlessly go off somewhere and hope he finds water. He sets out on foot to get there and then sees that the sheep get there. He provides the water for the thirst of the sheep. He makes that provision. That is the steering and the guidance of the shepherd. What is the state of this water? David described it as, "the still waters." I have mentioned this before, but it's important here, too. There is something about this water being still. Sheep will not drink out of rippling, noisy water. They will not drink water that is not clear enough so they can see themselves in it. It has to be still and reflect like a mirror. They have to see in there. They do not like to drink if they cannot see the bottom. They think there may be something they do not need, that would not be good for them.

So it is still water. This still water is water that they can see themselves in, calm; they can look in and see everything in it. If they can see clearly everything they want to see, they drink. That is the kind of water sheep have to have. What is the symbol of this water? Well, what does water symbolize in the Bible? It symbolizes two things in the Bible.

First of all, water symbolizes the Word of God. Ephesians 5:26 says, " . . . the washing of the water by the word." So, it is the Word. There is a reason they want the water to be clean. Remember in the Old Testament, Moses took the looking glasses, the mirrors of the women. They were brass, burnished brass and you could shine them until you could see yourself in them.

He took that brass and built a laver. It was a pretty big laver. Then he put water in the laver. When you came there to the water in the laver, you looked in it and saw yourself. It is the Word of God that reveals you to yourself. James called it the perfect law of liberty. It reveals the culprit, our selves. Just keep stooping to look, stooping and stooping. The more humble you get, the closer you get to the water, the better you see yourself. The sheep could look at that water and see themselves and know there was nothing wrong in there. They saw themselves in clear, calm water. The Word of God shows us what we are like. Sometimes I look at it and I do not like what I see. It looks tough. Sometimes it really does expose me. Yes, we can get very upset when we look at ourselves in a mirror. If we can look at the Word of God all the time and never find anything wrong with us, we are not seeing something. The shepherd sometimes put the sheep in that water and washed them white as snow. When you try the Word, you will get clean.

The water clarifies. The sheep can see in that water and it lets them see things they could not ordinarily see. Remember, I told you in a previous chapter that sheep do not see well. The Word of God is the only thing that can help us see that which we cannot see without it. It clarifies for us. Sheep could see things in that clear water. They understood that it was all right to drink it, if they did not see anything wrong.

This water comforts also. It satisfies their thirst. There is comfort from that water. Remember what we wrote about the rod and staff? They comfort me. They are the Word of God, and the Holy Spirit. You just cannot do without the Word <u>and</u> the Spirit. You have to have both.

Second, the water symbolizes another thing, the Holy Spirit. Jesus said in John 7:37-39, " . . . If any man thirst, let him come unto me, and drink. He that believeth on me, as the scripture hath said, out of his belly shall flow rivers of living water. (But this spake he of the Spirit, which they that believe on him should receive: for the Holy Ghost was not yet given; because that Jesus was not yet glorified.)" Water many times in the Bible means the Holy Spirit. We cannot do without this combination. Every time we see the Word, we have to look in the water. The Holy Spirit lets us see in. He has to illuminate it for us. He has to open our minds. We cannot do without Him. We have two-fold water here - the water of the Word and the water of the Holy Spirit. The Holy Spirit illuminates the Word so we can see. The Bible is a light. To see this light, you have to have another light, the light of the Holy Spirit. He has to illuminate our minds. He has to break the Bible open to us.

God did not write translations. He just wrote one book and we have it. Born of the Hebrew and the Greek, God has used this book (KJV) to get the message of the Gospel around the world, and sold more copies of this one book than any other translation in the world. That is enough for me to stay with it.

Some say, "I can hardly understand it - the language." You could give them a million translations and they still would not understand it. Men do not understand this book with their natural minds. A man can have a dozen doctoral degrees and a 16-cylinder mind, but the world by wisdom knew not God, as I Corinthians 1:21 says: "For after that in the wisdom of God the world by wisdom knew not God, it pleased God by the foolishness of preaching to save them that believe." (Not foolish preaching.) Men will translate it, to try to make it simple, but it will still be void of the Spirit. The King James Bible is written in the purest English ever printed.

Look at the words some time. Just look at the words. How do you read them without looking at them? Look at them. This Bible, in the main, is written in one and two syllable words. Get your Bible out and start counting the one and two syllable words in one stanza, some verse of your choice. There are whole chapters in the Book written that way. One and two syllable words are the words little children talk. Your little child talks in one and two syllable words. It's just little simple words. For example, look at the words in Acts 7:55. Look at the words. "But - that's one syllable, he - one, being - two, full - one, of - one, the - one, Holy - two, Ghost - one, looked - one, up - one, steadfastly is three, into - two, heaven - two, and - one, saw - one, the - one, glory - two, of - one, God - one, Jesus - two, standing - two, on - one, the - one, right - one, hand - one, of - one, God - one."

You ask some people, and a bunch will tell you, you cannot understand it. And they are right as they can be, but not for the reason they think. You cannot <u>unless</u> the Holy Spirit teaches you. He is the one Who lets you see in the water, or see what is in the water. He makes the Word real to you. He is the one that supplies, and provides it to you, and makes it real in your life. He makes it active in your life.

When the sheep get the still water, their thirst is satisfied. To get your thirst satisfied, get in and drink it. Let God make a spectacle of you. Satisfy your heart. Then the Shepherd has been obeyed. The sheep followed their Shepherd to the water. "My sheep know my voice and they follow me." We have to go with Jesus to the Bible, go through it with Him by the Spirit, if we are to get what He has for you.

VII. THE SHOUT OF THE SHEEP ALL DAY IS "I SHALL NOT WANT"

That is a proclamation. That is really a shout. When David thought of the Lord, my shepherd, he just shouted out, "I shall not want." Here is what that proclamation of David as a sheep of God's pasture means. It is an expression of faith and trust. I have the kind of shepherd I can trust. He will provide everything I want. David trusted Him. If you have it, it came from the Shepherd. I hope you trust Him enough to follow Him. Not only is it an expression of trust and faith, it is an expression of rest. As they say in Jamaica, no problem, no worry, I shall not want. The shepherd wanted for the sheep to have rest. When sheep were satisfied with him, they did not know how to worry. No worry for the sheep. They do not have a worry when their shepherd's there, and they are fed. Worry is speaking with your emotions, and not your spirit. This proclamation is an expression of satisfaction. I cannot worry. I am totally satisfied. Complete satisfaction. David was even satisfied with everything the Shepherd did to him. He was satisfied with the providence of the Shepherd. The Shepherd sometimes had to carry him through the valley of the shadow of death where everything was dangerous. He did not complain about it. He was satisfied with it.

Psalm 118:24 is one of the best-known verses in Scripture: "This is the day which the Lord hath made; we will rejoice and be glad in it." We need not complain about God's providence in our life. When we do we are complaining against God. David knew satisfaction. One other thing: this proclamation is an expression of courage. "I shall not want." David said there was not any fear there. He was not afraid with his Shepherd.

These are the first two (and the most important) provisions the shepherd makes for his sheep - the pasture and the water. With these, you have combined the Word of God and the Holy Spirit in your life. You cannot do well in this life without both of them. We have to have them both before we can say from the heart, "I shall not want."

Curtiss F. Lee, TH. B., TH. D.

Chapter Fourteen

THE SHEPHERD'S RESTORATION OF THE SHEEP

"He Restoreth My Soul"

"He restoreth my soul." (Psalm 23:3)

I. WHAT DOES RESTORATION MEAN?

The shepherd's restoration of the sheep or, if you will, the people, is a spiritual restoration. Christians are human beings and therefore are imperfect. There has never been a Christian who has not at some time or other needed a restoration. The person who has never had a restoration could be a lost person. You cannot restore a lost person. You cannot refurbish that which has not been furbished. You cannot renew that which has never been new. You do not rebuild new buildings. If you have never been stored, you cannot be restored. You know that restoration is a word that has to do with backsliding and backsliders. A lost person has never been anywhere to backslide from. He cannot backslide. He has never been to God to backslide from Him. That is what God meant when He said His people are a backsliding people. You cannot have a lost man restored. He has to be born of the Spirit, first. He has to come to God first, and be saved. Then he might fall away and be restored.

For Christians, restoration is needed every day. If you never had any need in your life, never realized any need of restoration, any sense of the need of restoration in your life, I question whether you are saved or not. There is no way for a shepherd to take care of his flock without him doing a fundamental work of restoration. He continues to carry on restoration. It is a very necessary and fundamental work of a shepherd in relationship to his sheep. It is absolutely essential. There never was a time the sheep could do without restoration. They had to have this restoration in their lives. This very verse of scripture points that out.

"He restoreth my soul." The meaning of the word restoration is a "turning back to." That is the essential meaning of this word. To restore is to turn back to. When the sheep go off, the shepherd turns them back to the shepherd, turns them back to the flock, turns them back to the fold. Then it means also "to cause to go up." The scripture puts it this way in, Jeremiah 30:17, "For I will restore health unto thee, and I will heal thee of thy wounds, saith the Lord; because they called thee an Outcast, saying, this is Zion, whom no man seeketh after."

To cause to go up to, means to go up to the former health you had. Back to the former level of health, to be where you were at one time, when you were in good health. It means to cause to go up to a certain point, where you were at one time in health.

It also means, "to make pearly white" - everything made white between the shepherd and the sheep. David put it this way when he repented in Psalm 51:7, "Purge me with hyssop, and I shall be clean: wash me, and I shall be whiter than snow." The prophet Isaiah writes in Isaiah 1:18, "Come now, and let us reason together, saith the Lord: thou your sins be as scarlet, they shall be white as snow; though they be red like crimson, they shall be as wool." This also involves restoration. It means to turn back to. It means to cause to go up to a point of health where you were. You have moved away from that point. Restoration will get you back up to it. Restoration also makes everything pearly white in your life, as a sheep in relationship to the shepherd, and the other sheep. Let's look at the meaning of the word in relationship to the other sheep, and in relationship to the shepherd.

It means to lift back and up to the point and place where the sheep really belongs; to lift up and back to that very place and point in its health, its nature, its functions. In other words, bring the sheep back to its rightful and normal life as a sheep. It means to bring the sheep and restore it to fellowship - fellowship with its shepherd and the flock. "He maketh me to lie down in green pastures . . . He restoreth my soul." Understand that when you get restored, you are at least back to following Him. You are back in fellowship. Paul put it this way in Ephesians 4:23, "And be renewed in the spirit of your mind."

Then restoration also means "back to force." Sometimes a sheep gets weak or sick and loses strength. It means to bring it back to force of health and strength. It means also to bring it back to its function, all its normal functions. Sheep that graze in the pasture, drink the water, function in production of wool, fat, fleece, foals (lambs), and fluid (milk). Joy is not in the function. That comes with the shepherd, in fellowship with him. All is not function; keep that in mind. When we talk about restoring the sheep, we mean restoring the fellowship, force, strength, health and normal functions.

We are the people of His pasture. We are His people and sheep of His pasture. That has to do with us. When we get out of function and go astray, He has to perform the work of restoration.

II. WHAT MAKES RESTORATION NECESSARY?

A condition of the sheep necessitates restoration. A sheep can get in one of five conditions that necessitate restoration. Any one of them will necessitate restoration. I will point them out to you in the Word of God.

Any one of these conditions will make it necessary that the shepherd restore the sheep.

1. Scattered sheep. Sometimes the whole flock is scattered. Then the whole flock has to be gathered together. Ezekiel 34:12 says, "As a shepherd seeketh out his flock in the day that he is among his sheep that are scattered; so will I seek out my sheep, and deliver them out of all places where they have been scattered in the cloudy and dark day." Whenever a flock of sheep gets scattered, their shepherd goes among them, in the best place he can, in the most central place where he can reach them with his voice. He will start calling out by

name each one of them, standing in the most central place where they are scattered. One sheep will hear his voice and he will come, then another and another. He gets his flock back together. He makes it a flock again. It is not a flock when it is scattered. You cannot have a flock until it gets localized. The world church we hear about is not the church of the Good Shepherd. For it to be a flock of the people of God's pasture, it must be local.

The world church today has no answers. You cannot even assemble it. When the shepherd's sheep are scattered, when a whole flock just up and scatters, he stands right among them as close as he can and makes his voice sound out. His sheep hear his voice, and they come to him. He gets his flock back together. That is a necessary work. So many times over in the Holy Land you had sheep scattered by wolves. We still have the wolves scattering the flocks today, too. The wolves in the midst of the flock are what we have to watch for, wolves that are trying to draw away sheep for themselves to build a bigger name for themselves. A shepherd has to be ever alert or a wolf will scatter his flock.

One of the greatest things about the Christian life, I think, it that it is the greatest miracle in all of the universe. It does not matter what miracle you have listed as the greatest miracle. What astounds me is that the Holy Spirit can bring into unity all the different, divergent personalities in a church. Every one is different. One likes this, while one likes that. Yet, put them together and they can be made to harmonize. Unity of the spirit is getting Christians together. They even live together. How they do is a miracle. The shepherd makes it his business to restore the scattered flock.

2. Stubborn sheep. Isaiah says in Isaiah 53:6, "All we like sheep have gone astray; we have turned every one to his own way; and the Lord hath laid on him (Jesus) the iniquity of us all." That is talking about the willfulness of some sheep. In almost every flock there was some sheep that was stubborn and just insisted on its own way.

Somewhere in Australia a shepherd wrote about the finest ewe he ever had. She was a slick ewe. Always produced the finest sort of wool. But she had a bad habit of getting through the fence of the fold, and she taught every one of her lambs to do it. Then some of the other flock began to get through the fence. She led them. You know sheep follow sheep. He could never break her of it. So as much as he hated to, he made lamb chops out of her. When you are stubborn, the Great Shepherd teaches you. He chastises you. When you get willful, you are just asking for the Shepherd to take His rod and give you a good licking. That is restoration. He will bring you back to Him. He will break your will. You can be so stubborn that God will say, "All right, that's enough." He will just transfer you into His presence for chastisement.

3. Sick sheep. Sheep can get sick awfully quick. They can become anemic; they can get weak. I just showed you how he would restore them to health. The shepherd does that. We have many sick sheep in God's flock today. Some have a slow pulse. They have no zeal. They are not a bit zealous. They give out easily. Some think they are home, and do not realize they are not in the fold, but on a journey. Their breath becomes short and the shepherd cannot lead them very far before they need rest.

There are sheep that have a poor appetite, always sick. Some have no taste for the Word. They do not care anything about the pasture provided by the Shepherd. They have no taste for prayer. They have no taste for the study of God's Book. Some have no taste for teaching. They would rather chew a file than hear God's word taught. Some have no thirst and hunger for God; just a poor appetite. Some have crippled limbs so they cannot walk in the path of righteousness and the path of obedience. Some have faulty hearing. They have to stay close to the Shepherd, or some just will not hear the Shepherd. They will not hear Him about separation. They do not think it matters if they are separated. They will not hear about surrender, committing to His will. They will not hear about being humble. They will not hear Him about prayer. They do not want to hear about serving Him. They will not hear Him about being holy people. They hear only what they want to hear. Some have failing eyesight. They cannot see well. Sheep do not have good eyesight. Wolves get around them because they do not have strong eyes. They cannot penetrate like an eagle. They cannot make you out from a distance, either. The average person I know is like that, he cannot see beyond the end of his nose.

Seriously. They are not discerning. Moses "endured, as seeing him who is invisible (Hebrews 11:27)." God speaks things that only can be seen through the eyes of the Holy Spirit, looking into His Word.

They want something they can handle. They think that is real. Everything you can see about you is not real. It is temporary. It is what you see with the eye of faith that is real, and is evidenced by things not seen (Hebrews 11:1). Paul tells us in Hebrews 12:12&13, "Wherefore lift up the hands that hang down, and the feeble knees; And make straight paths for your feet, lest that which is lame be turned out of the way; but let it rather be healed." The shepherd was something of a doctor; and remember, our Shepherd is the Great Physician. The main thing He uses on His sheep is His oil. I will not discuss that much here since we have done so in another chapter. But read the Bible where it tells about the oil. It is good for the sheep and it heals them. The shepherd uses his oil to nourish them, nurture them, take care of them, and build them up when they get sick. Remember, oil is symbolic of the Holy Spirit.

4. Straying sheep. We have all gone astray. That means the sheep wanders off. The shepherd must bring the straying sheep back to himself, back to the flock, and back to the fold. He goes after it, keeps hunting until he finds it, and brings it back. In Psalm 119:176, we find the cry of a stray, "I have gone astray like a lost sheep; seek thy servant; for I do not forget thy commandments."

5. Sagging sheep. In the terms of the shepherd and sheep, it means the cast sheep. The word cast means to be cast down. I want to describe to you the condition of a cast sheep. It is one of the most pathetic conditions a sheep can get in. It is a sheep that is on its back with its

feet up in the air. Then while it is on its back, it is flailing frantically with its feet. Cannot get off its back. You have heard someone say, "I was flat on my back." This is where that saying came from. Flat on your back and cannot get up. It flails with its feet frantically, struggles to get over, and it cannot get over. It is helpless.

It lies there looking about, lashing about with its body, and it's frightened from frustration. That's a pathetic thing. The shepherd never likes to see that in a sheep. It bothers him greatly. This condition is not only pathetic it is perilous. While the sheep is lying on its back, you know what happens? His rumen becomes involved, gets full of gas, presses against the heart, slows down the blood flow, and all the extremities of the body go dead. The sheep grows cold and numb. The peril of weather makes it worse. If it is hot weather, that sheep will not live long. If it is cold weather, he might, but he might take pneumonia and die from that.

There is the peril of predators. Old buzzards will go flying around. They just know they are going to get a sheep to eat. They will find it, lying there, not dead but they will go to circling. That is how the shepherd lots of times finds the cast sheep; he sees the buzzards. Then the wolves come, and the lions look them up. They are just helpless on their backs. If being cast continues for long, there is the peril of death.

There are three causes of cast sheep. First of all, a sheep will sometimes look for, and lie down in, a soft spot that sort of fits its body, sort of an indentation. It likes to get comfortable. It will lie down on its feet, and they are not comfortable. Then it will roll over on its side, to try and get comfortable, and after a while, it rolls on over on its back to try and get comfortable.

Shall I apply it to Christians? You always hunt your soft place and your comfortable place in life. You're doing just exactly what that sheep does. You become cast down, and somebody will have to come your rescue. We go along, and we all want it easy and soft. We do not have the fortitude, the stamina and endurance of a real soldier. The sheep tries to get comfortable, and gets into trouble.

The Bible warns us about settling down. If you find that soft spot, you will become a cast sheep. Somebody will have to get you off your back, if you ever are to get off. Amos 6:1 says, "Woe to them that are at ease in Zion . . ." A second thing that is a cause for becoming a cast sheep is too much wool. The wool has grown long. That long wool has gathered up briers, rocks, debris of all kinds, and it will matt up with mud. That sheep gets heavy, and after a while it will lie down, roll on its back, and it has too much heavy wool weighing on it to pull itself back up.

There are two things I see involved here. Wool represents the sheep's life. It represents its own nature, because it is the nature of sheep that they grow wool. It also represents your old life, the life you lived before The Great Shepherd found you. God would not let the priests wear wool in His presence. Ezekiel 44:17 says, " . . . no wool shall come upon them, whiles they minister in the gates of the inner court, and within." You are a priest. If you are continuing to live the old life you are already cast. Cast is also represented by an accumulation of things for yourself, keeping it for yourself - keeping your wool, and not giving it away, holding on to it. We accumulate many things in our life. When we do, life begins to be lived for the things we have accumulated. We become cast down. We are already on our back, and are not aware of it.

Do you know what God meant for his sheep? Sheep are nomadic. They are pilgrims. They never get settled down. Do not drive your roots down too deep. Do not put more tent pegs in than necessary; you're moving on tomorrow. You are a pilgrim. You are a cast sheep if you are carrying too much of this world on your back. All the shepherd can do is take the shears and cut the wool off. That is the only way to handle it.

Then there is another cause for a sheep to get on its back and be cast down. It is too fat. The shepherd knows his old and fat sheep are neither the healthiest nor the most productive. The minute the shepherd finds a sheep is too fat, he puts it on a diet. He brings it back to health, to the right weight. Moses used the name, Jeshurun, to describe the people of Israel, when they were fat. In Deuteronomy 32:15, he says, "But Jeshurun waxed fat, and kicked: thou art waxen fat, thou art grown thick, thou art covered with fatness; then he forsook God which made him, and lightly esteemed the Rock of his salvation." In another place, Moses says, " . . . the people sat down to eat and to drink, and rose up to play" (Exodus 32:6.).

We have many cast downs. This is David talking about that very thing.

He sees the cast sheep. In Psalm 42:6 he says, 'Oh my God, my soul is cast down within me . . ."" When the sheep gets on its back, it has a sinking feeling, a frustration on the inside, and eventually it gets quiet. David said his soul got quiet. He was cast down. In Psalm 42:11, he says, " Why art thou cast down, O my soul? And why art thou disquieted within me . . .?" The most frustrated animal is a sheep on its back. It's disquieted. The shepherd has to find it, lift it up on its feet, and it has to walk with numbness in the legs until it can get to where it is walking right. The shepherd rubs its legs to get the blood circulating. Every time the shepherd turns it loose, it will stumble or fall. The shepherd will pick it up again, rub the legs again, help it along, until it is walking again. That's restoration.

III. THE SHEPHERD'S METHOD OF RESTORATION

1. The shepherd in person does the restoration. It must be done in person. Psalm 23 says, " He restoreth my soul." The shepherd initiates the restoration. He does not wait for some sheep to initiate it. He does not wait for a sheep to get healthy enough before treating it. He does not wait for a sheep that is gone astray to come back part of the way. He initiates the restoration. We would never get back unless He did. We do not know the way back by ourselves. What we need is not a little sympathy; we need restoration. He accomplishes it personally. We never get restored by an "it", or by a thing. The Lord Himself restores us when we stray.

   Some Christians think that if they could just get a little of the lighter side of life, get out and have a few pleasures, see or play some sports, go fishing, go on a retreat (which does not sound like Christian soldiers), they would get restored. Many churches have adopted these methods, in an attempt to restore strays. They have built a two-and–a-half-million dollar recreation building at one church I know, thinking that will restore them spiritually. Straying sheep are never restored by a thing, or by an "it." They never will get restored that way. It takes the work and the power of the Shepherd in your life to have true restoration. The Shepherd initiates it. He does not sit back in an armchair and wait for His phone to ring.

The shepherd still loves that sheep. It does not matter what condition the sheep is in. The shepherd is still observant and compassionate about it. He never goes after a sheep with an ugly attitude. He is broken up. His heart hurts. He goes out and restores. He will get rugged with a stubborn sheep, but he still restores it. That's what love does. Chastising it is an act of love. God's correction shows you love. Therefore, the shepherd initiates restoration.

"He restoreth my soul." He does not start out to do it, and then fail. He does it. That's His way. He will take the sick sheep and restore its health. The stubborn sheep he corrects and restores to obedience. He carries it, straightens it and restores it to obedience. He restores it to the flock and makes it one with Himself. The straying sheep, he restores to fellowship. The cast sheep, he restores to walk in the pathway. "He leadeth me in the path of righteousness." It is all in love. The Great Lord's work is what the shepherd does.

2. The means of restoration. What means does the shepherd use? His voice, his lamp, and his rod: put them together and you find every one of them represents the Word. His voice is His Word. The lamp is His Word. For Psalm 119:105 says, "Thy word is a lamp unto my feet, and a light unto my path." His Word, the blessed Son of God, can only console you by means of the Word. It has to be applied to you if you are to get restored. How would you be restored if you were not restored according to truth? Stray sheep have to come back by way of the Word of God. The Shepherd has to show us the way. He always uses His Word. He even feeds with His Word. Micah 7:14 says, "Feed thy people with thy rod . . . "

Combined with the Word, God will use the power of the Holy Spirit, Who is represented by the staff and the oil, to restore you. The staff is the way the shepherd united himself to the sheep. He would hook it around the sheep's legs or neck and lift it up to draw it to him.

The greatest symbol of the Holy Spirit in the Bible is oil. It is the most consistent. So it is by the Word of the God in the power of the Holy Spirit that the Shepherd restores his sheep. God does not have some other method. He will not pick out some pleasure or some recreation or some social engagement for you and tell you to go there and forget about your sins. He will get you with the Word of God and the power of the Holy Spirit when you get away, when you have gone astray.

That is why the sheep of God's pasture need to hear the Word. They have to hear the Word from the Shepherd. The power of the Holy Spirit, the staff and the oil enable lambs to come back, give them the strength to return. The Holy Spirit of the Good Shepherd brings them to the water to enlighten them. There is no other means of restoration besides the Word of God and the Holy Spirit. "Thou anointest my head with oil." That is the Holy Spirit. The Shepherd uses the oil to restore you to health. He puts it on your head to keep you from getting sunstroke.

Sheep get sunstroke easily in the Holy Land. Their heads are bare, between the eyes. The shepherd puts oil there. If he did not treat it with oil, the sun would give them sunstroke. This is the stronghold of the devil. In order for us to bring everything under the control of Christ and tear down the stronghold of Satan, the mind of THE HOLY SPIRIT needs to control our minds. Your mind will wander off like the mind of a sheep that it is, left alone in its thoughts. God's sheep can become sick in a mental way. Paul tells us in Philippians 2:5, "Let this mind be in you, which was also in Christ Jesus."

So it is the use of the Word of God and the Spirit of God that restores sheep in God's flock. In John 16:13, Jesus said, "Howbeit when he, the spirit of truth, is come, he will guide you into all truth . . . " The truth is the Word of God and the Holy Spirit is the third Person of the godhead. He is the only one that can apply that Word to me and you to bring us back to health, strength, obedience and fellowship with Jesus Christ. He is the only one.

IV. THE SHEPHERD'S PURPOSE IN RESTORATION

That purpose is two-fold in the Bible.

1. It is for the safety of the sheep. The Shepherd knows that a sheep out by itself is in danger. It will not be long until the Shepherd is out after it. I have listed the dangers and the perils. They are all out there, in the world where we live. We are in such perils it is impossible to live for Christ Jesus by oneself. He, THE GOOD SHEPHERD, has to secure us. He has to be our stronghold. He has to keep us. So, restoration is for the safety of the sheep.

2. He restores the sheep for the honor of the Shepherd. "He restoreth my soul." A shepherd that would not go after a straying sheep disqualified himself as a shepherd in biblical times. He was looked upon as an idle shepherd, a false shepherd. Other shepherds would not have fellowship with him. He had dishonored himself. His name would be worthless. We used to say that a man's word and his name stood for something. Well, a shepherd's name stands for something as well. Our Shepherd will not let any thing reflect on His name. He keeps us in mind. He will bring His sheep back to spiritual life when fellowship has been broken with Him. Our spiritual welfare and eternal destiny are bound up in the honor of Jesus Christ. Our Great Shepherd will not let us fail because His honor is at stake. You are a dishonor to the Shepherd if you stray from Him. You are a stubborn sheep if you will not hear. You may be one who is a cast down sheep, and you are lying on your back. You are being a dishonor to your Shepherd, if you are. You are stepping on His name, and that is His business. That is why He is going to bring you back, for the honor of His name.

    Philippians 2:9-11 says, "Wherefore God hath highly exalted him, and given him a name which is above every name: That at the name of JESUS every knee should bow, of things in heaven, and things in earth, and things under the earth; And that every tongue should confess that JESUS CHRIST is LORD, to the glory of God the Father."

Chapter Fifteen

THE GREAT SHEPHERD'S LEADERSHIP OF THE SHEEP

"He Leadeth Me"

He maketh me to lie down in green pastures. He leadeth me beside the still waters. He restoreth my soul. He leadeth me in the paths of righteousness for his name's sake." In these three verses, David talks twice about the leadership of the shepherd. "He leadeth me beside the still waters. He leadeth me in the paths of righteousness for his name's sake." In the last chapter, I discussed how the shepherd restored the sheep for the honor of His own name. Notice in the above verse David recognizes this truth, "for his name's sake. (Psalm 23:1-3)

There are three things that sheep cannot do without. They are always in deep need of these three things. They must have food (pasture), water, and guidance. They cannot do without any of the three. In this chapter we will focus on their need for guidance. You just cannot turn sheep loose by themselves and expect them get along. They never will get along by themselves. If they do not have problems getting to the grass or to the water, they still have to get through the valley of the shadow of death. Somebody has to get them through. They did not turn sheep out in the Holy Land where David lived, and Jesus lived. They would not survive. The enemies would kill them, or the thieves would steal them. They would be scattered, and the wolves would tear them.

I hear some folks say, "I do not need to pray," or "I do not need fellowship," or "I am a good man." You need all the help you can get from God and everybody else to get through this mess that Christians live in. You cannot do without the guidance of the Great Shepherd. Sometimes we might think we are adequate, but we are not. So in this chapter we are dealing with the matter of the Shepherd's guidance, the Shepherd's leadership of the sheep.

In the scripture above, these verses about his leadership, there are three major elements. First of all, there is the leader. The shepherd is the leader, not some sheep in the group but the shepherd. He furnishes all the leadership. Second are the led, (the sheep); they follow. Third, is the leading, the paths that are taken.

I. THE QUALIFICATIONS OF THE SHEPHERD AS A LEADER

Certain qualifications are required if you are ever to lead people, the sheep of God's pasture, correctly.

1) The shepherd must have Perception. He must have perception in the sense that he has a thorough knowledge that qualifies him to lead his sheep. He must first know that a sheep is his. Jesus said, "I know my sheep." He must understand them. He must know how far he can lead them at a given time. He must know if they are doing well in their growth. He must know all about the sheep. He has a perception about them, if he's qualified. We have studied the Scripture, so we know that God knows everything about us. Some times we just say God is omniscient, instead of going on and on about what He knows. In Genesis 16:13, it says that Hagar called the name of the Lord that spoke unto her, "Thou God seest me."

That is what qualifies Him to be your Shepherd and qualifies Him to guide you. He knows all there is to know about you. There is not a thing in the world about you that is hid from your Shepherd. He knows you like an open book. He can read you; He even says He knows your thoughts before you get them. We have a great Shepherd that is certainly qualified, from the standpoint of knowledge.

The shepherd must not only know the sheep but he must know what is good for it - what kind of grass, what kind of water, all its needs, and wants. He must know the right path to lead the sheep in. Over in the Holy Land, there are direct paths that lead to water, or to the grass. Off those paths are others that lead off because some animal, or some sheep, went that way. It may be into a cave and no further. If a shepherd got on one of those, he might even take them on a detour, or a bypass, to a place where the sheep could not cross. But he knew the right paths. God made Moses be a shepherd 40 years in the wilderness, as we have noted before, so he could learn all about it, because He was to use him to lead His people for 40 years in the same wilderness.

Where Moses took care of the sheep in that wilderness for 40 years, he learned every sheep trail. He knew how to get to the different places. He knew the way. He knew how because he was trained for it. He had walked that place. When he returned there with the children of Israel, he knew where to carry them. Our shepherd knows the paths. He knows. There are many things in life we do not know about, where we have to travel, the things we will go through. He knows all about them. He knows also where the paths are. He knows when we should pray. He knows where the water is. He knows how much a sheep can bear. That is why He comes along and picks the lambs up and puts them in His bosom. That is why He goes gently when the ewe has had her lamb. That is why He carries the crippled one. He knows exactly how much they can bear. You will not have more put on you than you are able to bear. I Corinthians 10:13 says, "There hath no temptation taken you but such as is common to man: but God is faithful, who will not suffer you to be tempted above that ye are able; but will with the temptation also make a way to escape, that ye may be able to bear it."

He knows all about the sheep's journey that will transpire by the end of the day. He knows the weather. He has been there, and watched those elements, and he has become familiar with them, he knows when a storm will strike. He knows when it is going to get too cold. He knows when it is going to be too hot. He knows the circumstances. In fact, he just about controls the circumstances, and of course, our Great Shepherd does as well.

All the circumstances in your life, He knew about before they came or will come to pass. That is in His foreknowledge. You call them circumstances; He calls them providence. There is not one thing that ever transpired in your life that was not there with the knowledge of God. It is His way of operating.

He knows all the enemies. He is very familiar with the reality of the lion, bear, and leopard. He knows their ways. He understands their strategies. He knows everything about when and where they will strike. He knows where the wolves are. He knows about the viper that He has to grab. He is prepared to protect his sheep. He therefore will not be taken by surprise. He is ready for them by His knowledge. He takes His sling, His club, His oil, and He is ready to meet them.

Our Great Shepherd met the enemy, the devil, and beat him on the cross of Calvary. All his demons, every demon in the universe, the Bible indicates attacked Jesus Christ, and the Scripture says He stripped them all. He has met every one of them. He knows your enemies, our Good Shepherd does.

He knows also the whole pilgrimage of your lifetime. He knows the end from the beginning and everything that lies in between. When the shepherd started out in the morning, he knew where the valley of the shadow of death was going to be. He knew they were going through it before the day ended. He knew his job, and he was ready for it. He was prepared.

The Great Shepherd has a perfect perception of sheep and their needs, and He knows the way to get them in the eternal fold. Jesus said in John 10:28, " . . . and they shall never perish, neither shall any man pluck them out of my hand."

2. The shepherd must have the Power to lead. That means he has the ability to lead. A shepherd is strong. Read about David, taking his bare hands and killing a lion and a bear (I Samuel 17:34-36). Just the nature of the work he did would make him strong. He would walk and walk, and then he would have to carry the sheep in his bosom, or a sheep on his shoulder. He many times had to wrestle with heavy rocks to make a way for a sheep to go. He was strong and mighty. He faced the hardships of a shepherd's life. He could not be a weakling. He had to be qualified in power. He had to have power to defeat the enemies of the sheep.

The Lord Jesus Christ, our Good, Great, Chief Shepherd had all powers given unto Him (Matthew 28:18). He has been empowered with all the power of Almighty God (Hebrew, Elohiym). That is the name by which God revealed himself to the patriarchs, prior to the time of Moses (Exodus 6:3). He has sufficient power to see us through this life, and the life to come. Sometimes, instead of listing all of His powers, we just say he is omnipotent. In Exodus 17:15, Moses called the name of the Lord that had given Israel the victory over Amalek, Jehovah-nissi, meaning "God is my banner." Moses built an altar in the desert after this victory, symbolic of the Lord's name, Jehovah-nissi. He has the ability, He is able the Bible says. He has total ability to take care of the sheep for the journey of life.

Remember our Shepherd is not some butterfly catcher, completely tender; yet He can be tender, even though He is the Lion of the tribe of Judah, before Whom the whole world freezes at the sound of His voice. In order for a shepherd to lead, he has to have the power to lead. David had the power, as a forerunner of our Shepherd, to take care of the earthly job of shepherd. Remember he killed Goliath. He also mentions in Psalm 18:34, " . . . that a bow of steel is broken by my arms." A shepherd had to have power in the Holy Land.

3. A shepherd must have the Provisions necessary to lead. There are seven of them, and the number 7 means perfection biblically. There are the scrip or knapsack, the oil, the lamp, the sling, the flute, the rod, and the staff. That means the shepherd has perfect provisions for his sheep. When the shepherd starts out in the morning, that shepherd will not go one step away from the fold until he has all of the provisions with him, provisions to meet any need that may arise in the life of a sheep. Every day he had them with him. I did not mention his cloak, but he even used that. That is the new life. That is the Holy Spirit. That is resurrection ground. If you count that, then there were eight provisions. The shepherd could pick up a little sheep, put that sheep inside, wrap it up next to his body, carry him, and get him warm. He did not let anything get by him. He had to have the provisions in order to take care of the sheep.

A shepherd had to be delighted to be a shepherd of sheep in the Holy Land in days gone by. He went out thoroughly prepared. He had all the provisions accessible to him, every shepherd did. Well, God said that He would, and He has freely given us all things in Christ. The Great Shepherd has everything we need. This is where the characteristics in the names, Jehovah-roi (God considers, or regards) and Jehovah-jireh (God will provide, or see to it) are applicable. (Jehovah-jireh is the symbolic name given upon Mt. Moriah.) The shepherd does not give us all the provisions at once. We do not need them all at once.

For example, you probably have heard this statement over and over,

"When you come to death's door, God will give you dying grace." Well, while you are living, you do not need dying grace, you need living grace. I expect you would find it more difficult to get along without living grace than dying grace. It is harder to live with the Lord than it is to die in Him. God knows what you need at the time you need it. If a sheep needs the staff, the Shepherd will use the staff on it. If it needs oil, He puts oil on it. If it needs light in the nighttime, being a stray, he has the light to get it in. Each one of these provisions represents the Holy Spirit and/or the Word of God to the sheep of the Great Shepherd's flock.

4. A shepherd must have Passion and Compassion to lead. Jesus looked upon the multitudes and was moved with compassion. No man was qualified to lead. They did not love the sheep. If a shepherd did not love the sheep, then he would not be out there long. A shepherd had to love them, even to the point of dying for them. Jesus said the Good Shepherd (and that is the One that loves you), " . . . the good shepherd giveth his life for the sheep" (John 10:11) Sheep get in more scrapes, cause more trouble, have more trouble, cause more sacrifice; you would not put up with them if you did not love them. These are the qualifications that make a man a shepherd: perception, power, provisions, and compassion. The shepherd had to have all four of them.

II. THE CHARACTER OF A SHEPHERD'S LEADERSHIP

Not only the qualifications of the leader, but also the character of his leadership is essential. What kind of leadership is it?

1. That leadership is Personal. It. Is fitted to the needs of the sheep. It is fitted to their individual natures. Here is how it's done. In the morning, he leads the sheep out early, while the dew is on the grass. That is what they need most right then. His leadership is fitted to that need. He led them to the grass as soon as he could while it was cool. While the dew was on it, the grass was more valuable. It would give

them more nourishment. At noon, or when it began to get near noon and it was getting hot, he would lead them to the shade of a big rock, or a shady nook where there was water and protection against the heat. The shepherd's leadership was according to the nature and the need of the sheep. Then when night fell, he took his light and went straight to the fold. He counted them in with his rod. He examined them with his rod to see if all were well. He would count them in one by one. If there was something wrong, he treated it. If there was one astray, he went after it. He always directed his leadership to the needs of the sheep, and their nature. The shepherd provided them a personal leadership. He did not just treat them as a flock. He fitted his leadership to the nature and needs of each sheep.

The Lord has done that. He came here, and became acquainted with you and me. He knows exactly what we have need of in our nature. Paul said in Hebrews 4:15, "For we have not an high priest which cannot be touched with the feeling of our infirmities . . . " He shared in our nature and our needs. He did not sin, but He took on the nature of man, and He cared. He fit His leadership to our needs.

2. The shepherd is Foremost in leadership. I mean by that, the shepherd is always number one. He is always the one in front. He is always out there. "He putteth forth his sheep, he goeth before them." He faces the danger himself. He meets what comes first. He is out ahead of them. He is standing between them and all the perils that could befall the sheep, ready to give his own life, if necessary. Well, that is what our Shepherd did.

The Lord Jesus Christ stood between us and the devil. He took all the sin, all our sin, on His own body on the cross. He went ahead of us. He set the pattern. He was first out there. If a shepherd was to lead, he had to get out first and foremost, and face everything that was coming. A real shepherd was obsessed with his leadership.

3. The shepherd's leadership must be Faithful. A hireling could not do

the work. A shepherd is always faithful to his own sheep. It does not matter what occurs - cold, heat, enemies, thieves, vipers, he is still responsible, and responsive to his sheep. He is always faithful to them. Even to the point of dying for them, if need be. That is what the Lord Jesus did. He was faithful in His leadership. You know you can follow Him, safely. He is faithful to you. He will not give you anything you do not need. He will stay with you. " . . . I will never leave thee nor forsake thee"(Hebrews 13:5). In Greek the word is in triple form: I will not, I will not, I will not leave thee nor forsake thee. That is an oath, for His name's sake.

4. The shepherd's leadership must be Final. By that I mean that the leadership of the shepherd is a final, unarguable thing. It is authority with the sheep. They never argued with him about it. The Lord reveals what He wants to reveal; what He wants us to do and be. Some people say, "I need to pray about that." What many who say that are trying to do is think of a way to get out of it. We are not to even pray about it, if we know we have the Lord's leading on something. I do not mean we have no need to pray, but we need to follow the directions set out in God's Word. That is where leadership is final. He is the authoritative one. He does not stay out in front of the fold, and say, "All right, sheep, I will let you decide where I am going to lead you today." Not on your life. No, He will not say, "Raise up your hind leg." He did not ask the sheep. Old, stubborn sheep do not like that kind of leadership. But it is our business, our obligation to follow Him. His leadership is silent.

Once the Lord Jesus starts down the way, you and I need to accept it and get to obeying it. We need to go after Him and not argue about it. We will get astray, get behind, something will happen to us, and He will take His rod and chastise us. His leadership is final. Paul said in Romans 8:14, "For as many as are led by the Spirit of God, they are the sons of God."

III. THE QUALIFICATIONS OF THE SHEEP THAT ARE LED

Notice what David says, "He leadeth me." He is the next one, the one who follows. The Great Shepherd, the Lord Jesus Christ, He is the leader. That is always so in the case of the sheep, the shepherd is the leader. This is what that means. The sheep are to follow. They never go ahead. They follow. The sheep are led by the shepherd. They follow him. There are three things that are essential in the life of sheep that follow the shepherd:

1. The sheep must be Obsessed with their shepherd. Obsessed with him. Jesus said in John, Chapter 10, that sheep will not follow a stranger because they don't know his voice. They are obsessed with that shepherd. They are devoted to him. They have an obedience to him. They are not following just a shepherd. They are obsessed with him, their shepherd. They love his voice. For you and I, that is the Bible.

2. The sheep must be Observant of their shepherd. They keep their eyes on him. Sheep see that shepherd even when they are grazing. They are always looking at him, trusting him, and depending upon him. The Bible says we are to be "Looking unto Jesus, the author and finisher of our faith . . . " (Hebrews 12:2). If you take your eye off the Shepherd, you are going in the wrong direction. If you are not looking at Him, you are not going with Him. You are going some other way. You are looking at something else, or someone else.

    I have seen the joy of men that have kept their eyes on Him; it is without description. That reminds me of that old hymn, "Joy Unspeakable and Full of Glory." Sheep do not see well, physically. They cannot see at a distance. When they are close to him, they can see him. They observe him. We cannot see any better, spiritually. We need to stay close to our Shepherd.

    The sheep must be Obedient to their shepherd. They must obey him. They have to keep on following him. Sheep are not smart animals.

There are three things about them that sure qualifiy them to follow:

A. They have an instinct in them that is natural from the standpoint of following. Instinct just works. It is just natural. Like a person that has been born of the Spirit, and becomes a part of God's flock, the sheep of His pasture. It is in his spirit and nature.

B. Besides that, they have an affinity for being led. They have an affinity for the shepherd. They are going to have him or they are not going anywhere. When I was lost, I did not have any affinity for Jesus or heaven. Jesus or heaven never entered my mind. Anyone who claims to have faith should have an affinity for heaven. The one that assigns you faith, Jesus, gave you an affinity for Him. We are like sheep that want their own shepherd. They will not follow a stranger.

C. They have an ability to be led. They just follow him with a dedication and a spring in their step. They have the ability for it. They are given to it, sheep are. They are real followers. What about you? There are all kinds of voices, all kind of false shepherds, all kinds of entertainment, all kind of interests, all kind of sports, and all kind of pleasures out there in the world - just thousands of voices calling to you. Are you weak in your faith and ability to see Him? Does anything get your devotion in place of the Great Shepherd, the Lord Jesus Christ? Well, you need to get a check-up. You might not be a sheep.

An old goat does not have the ability to follow anybody. He does what he wants to do. He will get right up on the ledge and walk in perilous places, on rocks that are the highest he can get to. He is a sure-footed being, proud and impatient. An old goat cannot be led by a shepherd. He has to be driven. A shepherd cannot help him. He will get out, jump the fence, and run off from the shepherd every time - but not sheep. Sheep just have an ability and affinity to hear the shepherd's voice and to follow him.

IV. THE LEADINGS OF THE SHEPHERD, WHICH MEANS THE PATHS

The leader "leads me in the paths of righteousness for his name's sake." These are the paths he leads us in:

1. The path of Righteousness. The path of righteousness means just walking in the right path. It's a path that is designed for walking; the one the Shepherd would have us to walk in. These are paths that are right, not paths that are wrong.

2. The path of Rest. "He maketh me to lie down in green pastures, he leadeth me beside the still waters." If He is leading, the path will lead to a place of rest. The Shepherd will see that the sheep get the right kind of rest. It does not mean that He will not lead us through the march of the pilgrim, and the walk of life. We may grow weary but He will get us to the place of rest.

3. The path of Refreshment. Sheep require much water and they have to have grass. They have to have prepared pasture. They have to have a cup running over. They get refreshed from these things.

4. The paths of Rigor. These are the hard tasks, through the valley of the shadow of death. The shepherd never wants his sheep to be soft and mushy. He wants them to be strong. He puts them through hard walking sometimes. There are plenty of rocks to get over, and hard hills and mountains to climb. That is the way of the Holy Land; it is a rugged terrain. It is mountains and hills and valleys and gullies. Therefore he put them in the path of rigor, hardship

5. The path of Progression. He is always leading his sheep in such a way, progressively to make them what they ought to be. He will lead them to the eternal home. He is leading them progressively. He does

not want his sheep to stay static; to just reach a certain state, and stop there. He wants to carry them on in progression.

6. Paths of Restoration. What is the purpose of the leading of the shepherd? Why do shepherds lead? Well, let me tell you why. It is for the Shepherd's name's sake. Psalm 23 in all its expression, everywhere, is an expression of a compound name of Jesus. His name involves all of this Psalm. There are seven parts in the compound name of Jesus, and yet it is all one.

A.   There is Jehovah-Rohi, which means, "the Lord our shepherd." The Lord, Jehovah; Rohi, my shepherd. Jehovah-Rohi.

B.   Jehovah-Jireh, which means, "the Lord our provider." "I shall not want." Every one of these verses is an expression of some part of His name.

C.   Jehovah-Shalom, which means, "the Lord, our peace." It says, he makes me lie down in green pastures, and I will not fear in the valley. I will have peace.

D.   Jehovah-Rophe, which means, "the Lord our healer." "He restoreth my soul."

E.   Jehovah-Tsidkenu, which means, "the Lord our righteousness." "He leadeth me in the paths or righteousness."

F.   Jehovah-Nissi, which means, "the Lord our Banner." He makes us victorious. He prepares the table in the presence of our enemies. He has won the victory for us. He keeps the banner of victory over us.

G.   Jehovah-Shammah, which means, "The Lord is there." He is the ever-present Lord. He is with me all the days of my life, and "I will dwell in the house of the Lord forever." We use the word, onmipresent, to say He is everywhere. Jesus used the words, "I AM" more than 10 times describing Himself, which means, "I am present, or I exist", in the Hebrew or Greek. They are the same words used by God in describing Himself to Moses (Exodus 3:14). Jesus said, "...Before Abraham was, I Am" (John 8:58), meaning that He had a presence, or existed. The Jews understood what He was saying, and accused Him of having a devil.

When the Shepherd in leading His sheep, getting them where He wants to, and taking care of them, His name and all these names are at stake. If He should fail, all of them will be dishonored. If He fails at any one of them, He dishonors all of them. Our Great Shepherd's leadership in this world, including His provisions for us, His getting us through the journey and bringing us to the eternal fold, has as its main objective to honor His name. God's Word is no good unless His name is good. His name is no good unless His Word is. Our salvation, our security, and all that God supplies are bound up in the honor of the name of Jesus. God will not fail to honor that name - all these seven names. Psalm 23 is the expression of the name of our Great Shepherd.

Chapter Sixteen

THE VALLEY OF THE SHADOW

Yea, though I walk through the valley of the shadow of death, I will fear no evil. (Psalm 23:4a)

There is an actual valley of the shadow of death in the land of Palestine. It is on the way from Jerusalem down to the Dead Sea, south of the Jericho Road. It can be seen at a distance, south of the Jericho Road, the valley of the shadow of death. Actually there is such a valley there. It is a very narrow, steep climb through a mountain range, where the water foams, roils, roars, and races over jagged rocks as it goes down that valley. It is a valley that is between rock walls, honeycombed, a valley of darkness and black caves, many caves. These are the places of wild animals, poisonous insects, deadly snakes, robbers and thieves. They hide in caves in the darkness.

The farther down you go, the darker it gets. Many of those walls are 1500 feet high - rock walls. It is a path that plunges downward from one end that is 2700 feet above sea level down at the other end that is 400 feet below sea level. It is a rugged place. Those walls are 1500 feet high and the widest place in that valley is 12 feet wide. It is <u>very</u> narrow. It is a hard place for a shepherd to take his sheep through to safety because dwelling in those caves and hiding in the darkness are the poisonous insects, deadly serpents, and the robbing thieves. If you have sheep going along the dark wall and you cannot see, an old thief can reach out of a cave and pull one in. It was not anything pleasant for a sheep to go through. It was real rugged.

The sheep must pass through the valley of the shadow of death to go to pasture. They must pass through it to return to the fold. Surely David had been through it many times. He carried sheep through it, and he got them safely through. God is turning that into spiritual truth in our relationship to our Good Shepherd.

I. THE MEANING OF THE SHADOW OF DEATH

It has a literal meaning. It means that in the darkness, in the caves and in the dens there were thieves that would kill the sheep. It did not mean the valley was dead. We have heard people say that some loved one went through the valley of the shadow of death, and died. This scripture does not refer to somebody dying. The sheep in this scripture do not die; they get through it.

It is a shadow. In those shadows are beasts that will kill the sheep. Death is there, and it is dangerous because they are right in the presence of those things that are producing death of the sheep, hiding in those dark caves and in the shadows of the night where strife can kill a sheep. They are right in the very presence of death as they go through. That valley is the shadow of death.

The spiritual meaning, of the shadow of death is something else. Look at the word shadow, for example. If you have a shadow, you must have a substance.

We cannot make a shadow without a substance. Without a body, we cannot make a body's shadow. We must have substance in order to have a shadow.

This is what the substance is: the substance of death is sin. The sting of death is sin. When Jesus died for us, He took out of death the sting of sin; but it left a shadow. I want to tell you something. The resurrection body will not make a shadow. It will have no sin in it. That means it will be perfect. If someone tells you they have not sinned for some period of time, just ask, "Then why is your body making a shadow?" Many will never think of that. It would not make a shadow if sin were not in it. Paul called our resurrection body a spiritual body in I Corinthians 15:44. In Hosea 13:14 we find these words, "I will ransom them from the power of the grave; I will redeem them from death . . ." Jesus has taken the sting out of death, which was sin. There is nothing left but a shadow. Isaiah put it this way in Isaiah 9:2, "The people that walked in darkness have seen a great light: they that dwell in the land of the shadow of death, upon them hath the light shined." Matthew used this same scripture in describing Jesus in Matthew 4:16, "The people which sat in darkness saw great light, and to them which sat in the region and shadow of death light is sprung up." This term (Shadow of death) is found in the Bible 20 times.

A shadow can frighten you or scare you. Being saved, we are still in the presence of death but it does not have substance for us. I Corinthians 15:55-57 says, "O death, where is thy sting? O grave, where is thy victory? The sting of death is sin; and the strength of sin is the law. But thanks be to God, which giveth us the victory through our Lord Jesus Christ."

Christ has left His flock only the shadow of death. Death does not have that old sting of sin in it any more. It was taken out. That is why David could say as he walked through the valley of the shadow of death that nothing would hurt him; "I will fear no evil." The Shepherd was there who had power over everything in that valley. Over all those thieves, over all the robbers, over the snakes, over the insects; he had separated and conquered them. David killed a lion, a bear, and the giant as a shepherd – with just his shepherd implements. When David slew Goliath he was slaying, as a shepherd, a type of the devil.

Jesus defeated the devil on the Mount of Temptation and in the wilderness. In the grave He took the power of death from the devil, defeated death, and rose from its clutches. He slew the devil and dispirited him who had the power of death. The devil is a defeated foe.

"Yea, though I walk through the valley of the shadow of death, I will fear no evil." Our Good Shepherd, Jesus Christ, left nothing but a shadow for us. He took the sting out. When we get our resurrected body, it will never make a shadow, because there will be no sin in it.

I know death will come to me some day, but all it will be is a shadow. The shepherd gets the sheep through all the dangers of death and even carries them through the shadow. They never pass through death, just the shadow. The Shepherd has power over death. He is there. Notice the change in pronouns from I to Thou, "I will fear no evil; for thou art with me."

II. THE CHARACTERISTICS OF THE WALK

"Yea, though I walk through the valley of the shadow of death." Look at those who walk. This is part of that pilgrimage. The sheep walk, but also the shepherd. It is the shepherd who leads them into the valley. I have overheard some folks say they never had any problem because they were following Jesus. They do not know what they are talking about. If the shepherd led the sheep into the valley of the shadow, the sheep did not go on their own. Jesus said, "In the world ye shall have tribulation . . . " (John 16:33). Do you know why? If you did not have tribulations, you would not have to depend on Him, and you would not want to be close to Him. The shepherd leads the sheep into the valley on purpose. God cannot make two mountains without a valley. You cannot stay on the mountaintop all the time. If you get off one, you go through a valley to get on the other one. He will carry you there.

1. It is a Difficult walk It goes from 400 feet below sea level to 2700 feet above, up where water is roaring, with ripping, jagged rocks and steep ledges. If you fell off one of them it would be sure death. There is nothing easy about it. You will not find a more difficult place to travel in this world. There are times, going from one level of rock up to a higher level, that the shepherd gets up but some of the sheep cannot, so he will help them. Sheep need help to walk on that journey. That is how difficult it is. We will not get through this life unless the shepherd helps, either. The Christian life is neither easy nor hard. But is totally impossible without the Great Shepherd. Jesus said, " . . . without me, you can do nothing" (John 15:5). We cannot do a thing that belongs to the Christian life or belongs to the spirit, without him. That which we do on our own is the flesh, and will not be accepted by God.

2. It is a Dangerous walk. That is why this valley is called the shadow of death. There are all the ferocious beasts, those destructive animals, that shrewd king lion lying in the rocks waiting for sheep, as well as the thieves, the killers, and the robbers. It is a dangerous walk. We do not know how many dangers God brings us through every day that we do not even see. Danger lurks on our pathway

every minute. This is a dangerous world we are living in, filled with all kinds of perils. If we are not close to the Shepherd it will be more dangerous.

3. It is a Directed walk. Those sheep cannot find their own way through the valley. They do not know where to turn. They do not know how to get over this rock or that stream. The shepherd absolutely gives them total direction. He directs their every step through the valley. This is the one time the shepherd makes all of his sheep get close to him. That valley is five miles long and if sheep are strewn out in a grazing file, 100 sheep or more, somewhere toward the end of that line, the lions and the bears are lurking. The shepherd pulls the sheep close to him, and directs every step they take. The Bible says, "The steps of a good man are ordered by the Lord . . ." (Psalm 37:23). If we are walking right, every step we take, God is leading. We need that direction. If He is not directing, you will make a misstep, and you are going astray. You will be in the wrong path.

    If He is not guiding, giving total direction, we are out of fellowship with Him. We are off on a tangent. We have gone wrong. If you are not righteous, He cannot order your steps, but the steps of the righteous man, He orders. He directs them.

    The children of Israel could not get through the wilderness on their own. God led them by the hand of Moses in a waste howling wilderness filled with serpents and scorpions. If Moses had not been trained by God as a shepherd, they still would not have made the Promised Land. God led Moses; he could not have done it on his own, either. God gave them direct orders, through Moses, and directed their path through that terrible wilderness. It is a directed walk.

4. It is a walk of Destiny. I want you to notice it. "Yea, though I walk through" - not merely into it and left there - but to walk through it. That shepherd had a destiny in mind. He was going to get them

through to that destiny. He was not going to leave them there. Jesus Christ never leads you into the valley of the shadow of death; goes off and leaves you to get through on your own. He will see you through. I think that is the greatest word in this scripture about this walk. There is nothing greater than "going through." We have that promise.

The complications and complexities of life are a confusing mess, but He will get us through. He will not lose us in the confusion. He will bring us through. The Great Shepherd will do that for us. Jesus said, " . . . they shall never perish . . . " (John 10:28). It is a walk of destiny. Thank the Lord! I am so glad I do not have to stop and figure out how to get through this thing by myself.

The fold is at the end of the journey. There is no way to get there, except through the valley. The Great Shepherd will get all His sheep through. Not a one of them fails. If one goes astray and 99 get in, He leaves the 99 with the porter, goes after that one, and brings it back through that valley of the shadow and puts it in the fold. It is a walk with a destiny.

III. THE COMPANION OF THE WALK

I want us to understand everything this scripture says. The shepherd's sheep is talking now.

"Thou art with me." Its companion is the shepherd. In this verse, there is a change in the personal pronoun. Up until now, when the sheep is talking about its shepherd, it sees a benefit for itself. "He leads me beside - he makes me lie - he restoreth my soul - he leadeth me in", - but see what the sheep is saying now. He's now talking to the shepherd. "Thou art with me." The lamb is talking to him personally. This journey has become personal. Now in this valley of the shadow of death, there has come a personal, close, intimate fellowship. I told you this would be the time the shepherd would keep the sheep closer to him than any other time in the day. He is going to have them with him, not in a file line. He has called them right around him. He has his staff in his hand so that when and if they should bolt, he will just pull them right in close. They will be around him. They are so close to him, they can just look up and say, "Baa! My shepherd, thou art with me."

This illustrates one of those double names for God in the Word: Jehovah-Shammah, the Lord is there. That is what it means. That is what this word is. "Thou art with me". Jehovah-Shammah. You are right here now. I am right in your presence. I am closer to you in the valley of the shadow of death than I have ever been. More than when I'm grazing in the grass, or when I'm drinking in the water. Thank God for His presence in the midst of the valley. He is right there with us, in the closest sort of fellowship. That is what he is talking about.

The Great Shepherd is with the sheep. It means that the almighty God is with the weak man. It means that the Creator is with His creatures. It means the sovereign is with His subjects. It means the infinite is with the finite. It means the divine is with the human. It means that the Holy One is with the redeemed sinner. There is fellowship, closeness, and protection. "Thou art with me." The shepherd is the sheep's closest companion in the valley of the shadow of death.

IV. THE COMFORTS OF THE WALK

That is the exact reality of our Shepherd. He provides us with the comforts we need.

1. Goodness. When you come to death's door, in the valley of the shadow, people can only go just so far with you. Have you ever felt helpless beside a loved one at death? It is not a pleasant thing. Dr. Avery Rogers said he looked his youngest brother in the eyes and said, "Son, the chips are down." (He had cancer of the spinal cord and cancer in the lungs, and the doctors had given him less than six weeks.) "I wish I could help you, but I cannot. I cannot go into that valley with you. But I know one who can." Then is when you need the Great Shepherd most, and He is closest to you. He can walk through that valley with you. That is what David needed, that kind of shepherd.

2. Mercy. We have been told that sometimes a shepherd had sheep dogs. Good names for them would have been, Goodness and Mercy. They kept the sheep headed toward the shepherd all the time. One called them the hounds of heaven. Jeremiah said in Lamentations

3:21-23, "This I recall to my mind, therefore have I hope. It is of the Lord's mercies that we are not consumed, because his compassions fail not. They are new every morning: great is thy faithfulness." Notice, goodness and mercy follow "all the days of our lives."

V. THE COMPLEMENTS OF THE WALK.

Certain things complemented this walk. David said, "for thou art with me; thy rod and thy staff, they comfort me."

1. The rod. The rod is the shepherd's club. I wrote about it previously; that it had a knob on it, made out of wood with metal nails or some sort of metal in it. The club is the shepherd's implement of warfare, his implement for conflict with the enemy. J. L. Porter wrote in "The Giants' Cities of Bashan," in 1867, that he observed shepherds that looked more like warriors than pastoral shepherds. They were armed with weapons of that day including daggers, pistols, long guns, and battleaxes.

   In this very valley where the enemy of the sheep is most prevalent, the shepherd needs his rod. He could see the eyes of a lion way down there. Before he ever gets to the lion, he could throw his rod with such accuracy that he could get him between the eyes, knock him out, and kill him. Or he could see that viper about to strike and he would strike first.

   I have told you what the rod is good for. It also means a scepter. The word itself means a scepter to rule. It means that it is power. The Word of God to us is our rod. The Word of the Chief Shepherd has authoritative power with the sheep, and it has power with the enemy, too. The Word of God is a great source of comfort while we walk this way. Psalm 23 has comforted millions of people since David penned it.

   A. The rod was used for Numbering purposes. The shepherd numbered the sheep with him when he went out and when he came in. God said to Israel in Ezekiel 20:37, "And I will cause you to pass under the rod . . . " He was going to count His sheep as He brought them back into the fold.

B.   The rod was used for Investigative purposes. In Psalms 139:23&24, David cried out, and he's referring to a shepherd's kind of investigation with the rod. "Search me, O God, and know my heart. Try me, and know my thoughts. And see if there be any wicked way in me . . ." Look me over completely Take your rod on me, part the wool and see if you find any scabs on my skin. I will not pull the wool over your eyes. The Word of God is an instrument that absolutely discerns you, and points out your scabs of skin.

C.   The rod had a Corrective purpose. He knows you're going to stray, so He will correct you with the Word. The Word will apply anywhere in life, but especially in the valley of the shadow of death. This is why David said it.

D.   The rod had a Protective purpose. The shepherd protected his sheep with it. That is why the David would say, "it comforts me." It is by the Word of God that we can be protected from our enemy. That is what he had in mind in the valley. We need that Word for protection.. The reason he was comforted was that he was protected from the enemy. Paul said in Ephesians 6:12-17, that we should put on the whole armor of God., including truth, righteousness, the gospel of peace, faith, salvation, and the sword of the Spirit, which is the Word of God.

2. The staff. The word staff here means a stay and support, something to lean on. A stay and support that strengthens you and saves you. To us it means The Holy Spirit. He is called the Comforter, which means a helper, a support and stay. Jesus said He would send another Comforter, like unto Him, who would be there in the nick of

time to help you, to save you, and to support you. The staff represents the shepherd. I cannot think of a shepherd apart from his staff. The Holy Spirit always glorifies and represents the Great Shepherd, Jesus Christ. The Holy Spirit was sent to speak of Jesus, not of Himself. If you are led by the Shepherd, you have the staff, the Holy Spirit, that makes the Shepherd the ruler in your life. He is talking to you about Jesus, not Himself. He is not talking about gifts, but the Lord, Who gives them.

The staff, representing the Holy Spirit, more than anything points to the Great Shepherd. When you see a man with a staff, you think of him as a shepherd. That staff shows him to be the ruler. The Holy Spirit marked the entire life of Jesus for us. He was born of the Spirit in Mary's womb. Jesus lived by the Spirit, and was raised from the dead by the Spirit.

The Holy Spirit will magnify Jesus. He is not going to magnify tombs and gifts. If you are magnifying the Spirit, you may find out you are under another spirit, not under Him. The staff represents the Holy Spirit, pointing to the Great Shepherd and carrying on His mission. The staff had many uses for the shepherd with his sheep:

    A.   Drawing the sheep close to him. When they went through that valley, he had them close to him. He could just reach over and pull one that was looking off the other way, trying to go another way, back into the way. He drew him to himself, and he drew him to the flock. Paul spoke of walking in the Spirit. When the staff was hooked to the sheep, it bound him to the shepherd. It is the Holy Spirit that binds us to and keeps us with Jesus. We need that Great Shepherd and we need every one of the other sheep as we go through the valley. We need that unity. We need all the help we can get.

    B.   Lifting the sheep. Sometimes the shepherd would have to get to a certain level. He would reach with his staff and lift the weak sheep up to him on the higher level. Some of the sheep were strong and could jump up. But there would be some that could not - little lambs or ewes or weaklings. If the Holy Spirit of God does not lift you to where God is, you cannot get there by yourself. He will lift you there.

C.   Directing the sheep. Sometimes when the sheep were walking in dangerous places, the shepherd would lay his staff to his side and direct them on their way.

D.   Disciplining the sheep. The shepherd could take the crook in his staff and put a hard jerk on a sheep if he did not behave. He might even tap him with it. For disciplinary purposes he used his staff to keep the sheep going where he wanted them to go.

E.   Comforting the sheep. "Yea, though I walk through the valley of the shadow of death, I will fear no evil for thou art with me. Thy rod and thy staff they comfort me." The sheep are comforted mainly in two ways:
- a. By the presence of the shepherd. "Thou art with me." That comforts sheep more than anything else.
- b. By the Word and the Holy Spirit. In this life if you are not living by the Word of God, then you do not have the Holy Spirit guiding you. You will not have much comfort in the valley of the shadow, without having the Comforter with you when you go through. You will be miserable. If you are not walking in that daily presence of Jesus, you are upset and disturbed. If the Word does not mean much to you, the Holy Spirit does not control your walk, and you will be frustrated.

VI. THE CONSEQUENCES OF THIS WALK

1. It eliminates sin. I fear no evil. Sheep are never afraid in the presence of the shepherd, even when he is using his rod and his staff. They do not know what fear is. They never fear if he is there. It is the rod and the staff being exercised.

2. It gives assurance of security. They are in the presence of their shepherd, with his rod and his staff. They know they are going into the valley, but they are going to walk through the valley.
3. It guarantees completion of the walk. It is a walk through, not into only to stop in some holding area. Walk through in the presence of the shepherd, with the powerful rod and the staff comforting the sheep. They are going through the valley of the shadow of death, all the way to the prepared table in the Lord's house.

Chapter Seventeen

THE PREPARED TABLE

Thou preparest a table before me in the presence of mine enemies: thou anointest my head with oil; my cup runneth over. (Psalm 23:5)

In the eastern countries, especially in areas of Palestine, we find that hospitality played a great part in their life. They wanted you to come to their home. If you did not go, it was an insult, a very serious insult.

They are people given greatly to hospitality. They liked for you to come and drink of their cup and eat of their food. In this part of the scripture it is something like that. He has prepared a table for me in the presence of enemies, anointed my head with oil, and the cup runs over. So quite a bit of emphasis on hospitality is given. Do not let that lead you off. This is still a pastoral relationship, a relationship of the shepherd to the sheep, and he is taking care of them.

The table might make you wonder what the scripture is talking about. But when you find out what it means, then it will clear up, because this is still about a shepherd and his sheep. There is not any change in the meaning. In Psalm 78:19,52-53 we find these words. "Yea, they spake against God; they said, Can God furnish a table in the wilderness? . . . But (he) made his own people to go forth like sheep, and guided them in the wilderness like a flock. And he led them on safely, so that they feared not: but the sea overwhelmed their enemies." I want to talk about two prepared tables, one in the wilderness and one in the hereafter.

I. THE PREPARER OF THE TABLE

Notice David says, "Thou preparest a table before me." He is talking to the shepherd. Not some church, not some political system, but the shepherd. He was there with the sheep.

1. The shepherd is Qualified.If you will look at him you will find that the shepherd is qualified to make preparation of the table. For example, he is knowledgeable about the rules, regulations, and requirements of the guest. He is knowledgeable about the circumstances at and around the table, whenever he is ready to have the sheep get on it. He is adequate in his preparation. He leaves nothing undone. He gets the table set for the sheep; it is ready. He makes sure the preparation of the table is adequate.

2. He is very Gracious. He leads the sheep to their places at that table, when they come to eat that which he prepared.

3. He is very Provident. He has made everything ready for them. He provided everything they need on that table. I should identify that table for you. I used to think it was a table he built out of material and put grain on it, but that is not the case. It was a tableland of grass. When the shepherd went on a mountainside with his sheep, he would head for a shady place where the mountain had shaded the grass from the hot summer. It would be green and flourishing. If it were winter, he would cut the limbs from leafy trees in place of grass, and spread them on the ground. This is that kind of table. It is called a tableland of grass.

The table had to be prepared before he would lead his sheep onto it. He made it ready. The way he made it ready was that if he found poisonous weeds, he would take his rod and beat them off at the ground, pick them up and carry them from the table area. Before the sheep began eating grass, he knew what was poisonous to them, and he removed it. That was part of the preparation. If there were lions or bears he ran them out. He would drive all the ravenous beasts off that table of grass.

One thing he searched for more than anything else was the viper holes. In that grass there would be viper holes. If a sheep got close to that hole, a viper would strike, and it could be dead in minutes. So he put oil around its circumference. Just made a ring of oil around the hole. The oil would run down the sides into the hole. Then that viper could not make it high enough to strike the sheep; it would slip back on the oil. Of course, when the oil was around that hole, the minute the sheep smelled it they pulled away. They would not get close to it. In that way it protected the sheep against the poisonous vipers.

He made preparation of the tableland of grass. What else is he talking about when you think about the preparation of the table? What is the table spiritually? We have already found out. Grass is symbolic of the Word of God. He prepared the Word of God. The Chief Shepherd, in the person of the Holy Spirit, gave it to holy men of old. II Peter 1:21 says, "For the prophecy came not in old time by the will of man: but holy men of God spake as they were moved by the Holy Ghost." He put it together exactly like He meant it to be. Every word of it is inspired, and every word of it is good for you. He made it ready for you. He prepared it. He knew your needs, before you ever got here. He looked down across time, and saw what we would need and he put it together.

He inspired this Book we call the Bible, what we call the King James Version, for English- speaking people. Some men think they are smarter than God; that they can make up their own Bible. That is what some are doing today. They are making their own Bible. They are making a tableland ready for the unsuspecting sheep. No doubt they have some of God's sheep eating on those poisonous weeds. Any time I go to a church, and the speaker begins correcting the King James Bible, I turn him off. Our Bible was originally called the AV, or Authorized Version, until men began correcting it. In order to give credibility to their work, they began to use the term KJV, to put it in the same category with their versions. They hate this King James Bible. But the Lord prepared it. This Book is still the champ of all times. It has been used of God, with God's blessings on it, more than any other translation in the history of the Bible. More people have been saved by it. More people have been called into God's work by it. Stay with the King James. It is the safest, purest, most beautiful English ever written, Victorian

English, in one and two syllable words for the most part.

Talking about understanding the spiritual truth, that's something else. It does not matter how many translations are available, many never will understand, unless the Holy Spirit opens their eyes and lets them see. The Lord has this one, the KJV, ready for you. He made the tableland ready. There is a harmony through this Bible that you cannot explain from the human or natural standpoint. It is utterly impossible. So He is the one that prepared, spiritually, the tableland, the Word of God. That is exactly where the Great Shepherd, in the person of the Holy Spirit, will lead you. You may be grazing on something poison if it is not a KJV Bible. Grass means the Word of God.

II. THE TABLE IS PREPARED IN THE PRESENCE OF ENEMIES

It is prepared in person by the shepherd. This is the point I want to make: he prepares the tableland in the presence of the enemy. There are enemies of your soul. They are enemies with determination. Rather than keep the shepherd from preparing it, he got it ready, while they looked on in amazement. David says "Thou preparest a table before me in the presence of mine enemies." You have enemies that will try to keep you from the table.

1. Vipers are an enemy. They represent the devil and demons.

2. Your own flesh is an enemy, your old self will. You do not naturally have gratification from the Word of God. You will need the Shepherd to lead you into it. Your flesh is a fighter, and it is at enmity with the Word. You will need somebody to help you onto the grass, and get the enemies out of the way.

3. The world is an enemy of the Bible. They do not want it around. They do not want you reading it. The spirit of this world will keep you from the table that the shepherd has prepared for us.

You have all kind of enemies about this tableland that will fight you every day, to keep you from it. Our flesh is against the Word. Do you have insomnia? There are people who cannot sleep at night. Do you have a hard time sleeping? I have a sure cure. When you cannot sleep, get your Bible and start reading. If that does not put you to sleep, start praying. The flesh and the devil do not want you reading the Bible or praying. If you have insomnia, just read your Bible. There are enemies against you reading the Bible. They do not want you ever to touch it. It has the Words of life in it. The world, the flesh, and the devil will try to stop your access to it. You have to have help from the Shepherd.

The Bible is <u>fact</u> to people of faith, who have faith in its Author. It records history, makes accurate prophecy, gives doctrine, and inspires to righteous living, because it is inspired. One example is Hosea 11:1, "When Israel was a child, then I loved him (past tense history at the time Hosea wrote), and called my son out of Egypt" (future prophecy). Jesus was carried to Egypt by Joseph and Mary, then called back, {Matthew 2:14&15). The Word is both doctrinal and inspirational, because these things are biblical facts.

III. THE SHEPHERD GUIDES THE SHEEP ONTO THE TABLE

When the shepherd gets the table of grass ready, this is how he gets the sheep onto it. He stands and calls each by name, one at a time, and he leads them onto it. He guides them onto it. I do not want you to forget that. If you ever get in this Word of God, you will have some guidance. In this day and time, the church age, the One who represents Jesus, the Holy Spirit, is the only One who can guide you into it. In John 14:26, Jesus said, "But the Comforter, which is the Holy Ghost, whom my Father will send in my name, he shall teach you all things, and bring all things to your remembrance, whatsoever I have said unto you." The shepherd did not drive his sheep upon the tableland. Nor did he give them the directions to the table where the grass was. He saw that they were all guided to the table before he sat down. You need divine guidance to the Word of God. It will take the Holy Spirit of God to guide you into the Word of God.

1. The shepherd guides you into all truth. II Timothy 3:16&17 tells us, "All scripture is given by inspiration of God, and is profitable for doctrine, for reproof, for correction, for instruction in righteousness: That the man of God may be perfect, thoroughly furnished unto all good works." The only way you will ever truly see it is by revelation from the Holy Spirit of God.

2. He will give you perception of the Word of God. He is your teacher. He is your theologian. He is the greatest teacher in the world, and you will have guidance to get into God's Word. The sheep were guided onto the tableland by the shepherd. We need the same guidance into God's Word. The Shepherd did it when He was here in person. He does it now by the Holy Spirit.

3. After the Shepherd gives you perception, you will need to develop it in practice. You cannot perform this in your own power. You cannot get it done in your own power.

There is not anything about the Christian life you can do by yourself. You will need God's Holy Spirit enabling you to live it.

There are things in the Word of God that just amaze me. I read where it says in I Peter 1:16, " . . . Be ye holy; for I am holy." We are to be just as holy as God. That knocks me out. I do not know about you, but I need some help here. I'm sure glad I have Someone Who can help. You are human, too. You will need some help here too, if you are to live to the standard set in the Word of God. You will have to have a power outside of yourself. Then He tells me to love my enemies. Be good to them. Bless them. Pray for them. I have not forgotten The Shepherd. He has met the requirements for me, and will enable me. Paul tells us in I Corinthians 1:30, "But of him are ye in Christ Jesus, who of God is made unto us wisdom, and righteousness, and sanctification, and redemption." I am in His body. Again, in I Corinthians 12:13 it says, "For by one Spirit are we all baptized into one body . . . " And in Galatians 3:27, "For as many of you as have been baptized into Christ have put on Christ."

Paul really knew how to take credit away from religionists who were trying to add some other door to the Father, rather than The Good Shepherd, Jesus Christ, who said he was The Door. I keep God's blessed Word always handy, to keep practicing. If you are to move onto the tableland The Shepherd has prepared, you will need help outside of yourself. We need to ask the Guide to guide us regularly, just to keep in practice of meditating on His Word.

IV. THE ANOINTED HEAD

The scripture mentions the anointing, and the cup running over. This is how that occurs. The shepherd has the table ready for the sheep. They are well taken care of. Then he takes them to the fold at night. At the door of that fold, the opening where they get in the door, he stands and he brings each sheep individually. He calls them by name, puts his rod on them so they cannot go in until he has thoroughly examined them. He looks to see if they have thorns in their flesh, or a rock in a hoof, or if one is sickly. He takes his rod and divides the wool to see if they have scabs that make them weak or sick.

Sheep can easily pick up fever in the day, in that hot country. Their faces will get hot. When he examines them, before he ever lets them go in the fold, you know what he does? He pours oil on their heads, because in the morning he has to get them out early to graze. They will be out in the hot sun before day's end. He will not have the time in the morning, because it would make them late to pasture. He puts oil on the head at night. He anoints their heads with oil. In the morning when he calls them out, their heads are already oiled.

Sheep need their heads anointed against the extreme heat of the sun in the Holy Land, or they may have sunstroke. So the shepherd anoints their heads at night. All the sheep get anointed.

This is symbolic for us. Oil is symbolic of the Holy Spirit. Always in the Bible, the oil is the most consistent type of the Holy Spirit, and it was to anoint your head. Psalm 45:7 says, "Thou lovest righteousness, and hatest wickedness: therefore God, thy God, hath anointed thee with the oil of gladness above thy fellows." The Holy Spirit is our anointing. We are anointed with the Holy Spirit for Jesus. "Thou anointest my head with oil." In Matthew 3:11 we find these words, (John the Baptist speaking), "I indeed baptize you with water unto repentance: but he (Jesus) that cometh after me is mightier than I, whose shoes I am not worthy to bear: he shall baptize you with the Holy Ghost, and with fire". Jesus does it. You get anointed. Those baptized with the Holy Ghost go into God's garner fold. The Shepherd puts the oil on the head. The anointing of the sheep is a very important matter.

1. It is for the purpose of purity. Oil heals wounds. It was even used by the patriarchs to treat the sick. It could heal up infections. It would

keep the sheep in spiritual health. It made a protective surface. Oil protected against sunstroke. That has to do with your mind. Did you know the Holy Spirit can give you a good mind? It is in the mind where you have trouble. This is where the devil gets his start. Paul said in Ephesians 2:14, "For he (Jesus) is our peace . . ." Again he said in Philippians 4:7, "And the peace of God, which passeth all understanding, shall keep your hearts and MINDS through Christ Jesus." That is why we need to think on the Word of God, feed on His prepared table; because our minds are the stronghold of the devil. Bible study will flush him out.

2. The devil will get in your mind and get it hooked on things that are not of God. He wants to keep you from thinking about Jesus. If you do not have the things about Jesus there, you will not have anything of Him anywhere else. The mind is of vast importance. It has to be under the control of the Holy Spirit like that sheep's head is under control of the oil to keep it from having a sunstroke.

It is for a preparative purpose. That means that when you anoint someone with oil, there is consecration to the Lord, there is a surrender to the Lord; and the journey, or the task that He has assigned him or her, consecration to Him. There is always an act of consecration.

3. A purpose of fellowship. You should have fellowship with the one you anointed in the Lord.

4. A jubilation purpose. Oil always indicates gladness. There is a wrong gladness, but the joy of the Spirit is what we are concerned about. When you are full of the Holy Spirit when He anoints you, you have a joy you cannot have any other way. It is jubilation. You will never be a joyous Christian without it. Jesus was a joyful person because He was anointed with the Spirit above measure.

V. THE OVERFLOWING CUP

"My cup runneth over." I have written about the oil - how the shepherd has a container of oil, really two kinds of oil. He also has a water container, which was usually a cup made from a goat's horn. Whenever the shepherd is ready to put his sheep in the fold, he gets the water cup. He always has it. He dips it in the water. He dips it in and fills it full. Sheep have a long nose and maybe this sheep has fever. Most of them will, from the heat of the day, with all that wool. They all march to the fold, and each sheep will stick its nose right down in there, right up to its eyes as the shepherd is inspecting it. The water will run out of the cup, an overflow. It will cool its face from the fever that it has. Then while in the cup, it drinks. It takes what is in the cup into itself. This is what is symbolic and applies to us.

1. The water in the cup can signify both the Word of God <u>and</u> the Holy Spirit. They are both called water in Scripture. Paul said in Ephesians 5:26 that Christ would cleanse his bride, the church, " . . . with the washing of water by the word." Jesus said in John 7:38&39, "He that believeth on me, as the scripture hath said, out of his belly shall flow rivers of living water. (But this spake he of the Spirit, which they that believe on him should receive: for the Holy Ghost was not yet given; because that Jesus was not yet glorified.)

2. Here is what I want to emphasize. First, there is a drinking. There is an appropriation of the water. There are many places in the Bible that talk about faith as eating and drinking. If you are to have this water in you, you have to appropriate it. You have to drink. You have to feed.

The Bible speaks of this in both ways, about it being the Word of God in you and also the Holy Spirit in you. Ephesians 5:18&19 says, " . . .be filled with the Spirit; Speaking to yourselves in psalms and hymns and spiritual songs, singing and making melody in your heart to the Lord."

Also, Colossians 3:16 says, "Let the word of Christ dwell in you richly in all wisdom; teaching and admonishing one another in psalms and hymns and spiritual songs, singing with grace in your heart to the Lord." When the Word of God came to you richly, the Holy Spirit came to you richly. When the Holy Spirit came to you richly and filled you, the Word of God came to you richly. They belong together. There is not any way to receive the power of the Spirit, except as the Word of God, or as God talks to you from His Word. They are bound together.

You have to drink of both of them. That is appropriation. It is not a one-time thing.

The shepherd put that cup out every day. They drank it slowly. Some talk about being filled once and for all time, but it really is always, every day. You have to appropriate both to yourself. You cannot keep from it, because you cannot store it. You are not like a camel that can carry weeks of water in his hump. You have to drink water every day. These two, the Word and the Spirit, are both like water to us. Appropriating both day by day is a necessity. Drinking is always an appropriation and it is done by faith. You can appropriate the Word and the Holy Spirit and have blessings in your heart now, if you will take them in, both of them. If you just keep on appropriating, the first thing you know, you will be overflowing. It is like a river of living water. You are not full enough, unless the Spirit is running over.

You might be just like the old Texas cowboy who said, "I'm full of old spiritual things. My cup has tadpoles in it." Yours might too, if you are not appropriating daily, in order to make it overflow and be filled anew. Your cup may be full of tadpoles. Your cup will go stale without a flow. That means, if you are full of the Word of God and full of the Holy Spirit, that kind of life will overflow and bless others.

I hope this explains the table in the wilderness. It was illustrated by Moses and the children of Israel in the wilderness, where God fed them with manna from heaven, and water from the rock, " . . . and that Rock was Christ" (I Corinthians. 10:4). We have compared the table of grass prepared by a shepherd for his sheep with the Great Shepherd, Jesus, feeding His sheep. He said He was the bread from heaven. John the Apostle also said He was the Word made flesh. Jesus told His disciples that He would be leaving, but the Father would send a Comforter in the person of the Holy Spirit. John 14:18 says, "I will not leave you comfortless: I will come to you." So we feed at the table prepared for us in this wilderness, on the Word (Jesus, the Bread of Heaven) and water from the Rock (God sending the Holy Spirit).

VI. THE TABLE IN THE HEREAFTER

Psalm 78:1&2 records these words of God, "Give ear, O my people, to my law: incline your ears to the words of my mouth. I will open my mouth in a parable . . . " This foretold some of the ministry of Jesus, Who spoke in many parables. A parable has hidden meaning to those without understanding. But Jesus said His sheep would understand His parables (Mark 4:11-13). Our comparison of Jesus and a shepherd is not a parable, but an allegory, which He applied to Himself in John 10:11 when He said, "I am the Good Shepherd . . . " The table in the hereafter is presented in allegory, parable, and in plain words of prophecy, mostly in the words of Jesus.

1. What is the table prepared for? In Revelation 19:7, we find it is for a wedding feast. The Scripture says, " . . . the marriage of the Lamb is come, and his wife hath made herself ready." Also, it says in Revelation 19:9, " . . . Blessed are they which are called to the marriage supper of the Lamb . . . " The wedding of Christ to His Bride, the Church, has already taken place when the hereafter table is ready.

2. Who will sit at this table? 1. In Luke 22:30 we find an invitation to the twelve disciples. Jesus, speaking to the disciples, said, "That ye may eat and drink at my table in my kingdom . . . "

3. In Luke 13:28&29, we find that the patriarchs and the prophets will be there. "Ye shall see Abraham, and Isaac, and Jacob, and all the prophets in the kingdom of God . . .and shall sit down in the kingdom of God . . . "

VII. THE FRIEND OF THE BRIDEGROOM, JOHN THE BAPTIST.

John 3:29 says, " . . . but the friend of the bridegroom, which standeth and heareth him, rejoiceth greatly because of the bridegroom's voice: this my joy therefore is fulfilled." I want you to notice the words of Jesus to His disciples in Matthew 26:29, " . . . I will not drink henceforth of this fruit of the vine, until that day when I drink it new with you in my Father's kingdom." So we do not start the party yet. The Bridegroom has not come for His Bride.

1. God's virgins. Matthew, Chapter 25 tells of the ten virgins, five wise and five foolish who had waited for the Bridegroom. The five that were ready for the Bridegroom went in with Him to the marriage feast, and the door was shut. Psalm 45:14 has a similar theme, "She (the Bride) shall be brought unto the king (Jesus) in raiment of needlework: the virgins her companions that follow her shall be brought unto thee." And in Revelation, Chapter 14, John tells about the 144,000 young Jewish men who become witnesses for Jesus during what is known as "the time of Jacob's trouble" or the tribulation period. Revelation 14:4 says, "These are they which were not defiled with women; for they are virgins . . . "

2. There will be other guests. Matthew 22:1-14 is a parable about a wedding feast. One ofthe guests that is called "Friend" is called out because he came without a wedding garment. I believe this refers to Judas, who was present when the invitation was given to the twelve disciples and Jesus called Judas, "Friend."

About the Bride Revelation 19:7&8 says, " . . . "for the marriage of the Lamb is come, and his wife hath made herself ready. And to her was granted that she should arrayed in fine linen, clean and white: for the fine linen is the righteousness of saints." We already know that we have been " . . . made the righteousness of God in . . . " (II Corinthians 5:17). Look also at the parable of the ambitious guest in Luke 14:8-14. Do not get impatient; the Bridegroom will come. To be there you must be a part of the Bride, His Body, the Church. The invitations are sent to guests, but the Bride comes with Him.

In Matthew 24:30, Jesus says, " . . . and they shall see the Son of man coming in the clouds of heaven with power and great glory." Here He is coming for His Bride to take her to the marriage feast. If you are not yet a part of the Bride, His Church, you still have an invitation to be a guest, given in the last chapter of the Bible in Revelation 22:17, "And the Spirit and the bride say, Come. And let him that heareth say, Come. And let him that is athirst come. And whosoever will, let him take of the water of life freely."

Curtiss F. Lee, TH. B., TH. D.

Chapter Eighteen

JOURNEY TO
THE ETERNAL FOLD

"I Will Dwell"

Surely goodness and mercy shall follow me all the days of my life. And I will dwell in the house of the Lord for ever. (Psalm 23:6)

The journey and final destiny of the sheep/ The pilgrim's journey to the final abode.

Sheep are nomadic animals. That is, they travel all their lives. They never get where they are bound and stay at one place very long. Even the fold they have at night is temporary. They do not stay there except for a few hours. They get in after dark. The shepherd is up early and they leave. Nights for a sheep and his shepherd in the Holy Land are short.

They are up early, out to the grass early. In the hot time of the day, they are lying by still waters in a nook that is shady and cool. They are nomadic, traveling animals. They are pilgrims. Since we are pilgrims in this world, I like to say, "Brother, don't drive your stakes down too deep here. We're moving in the morning." Keep that in mind. The sheep of God's pasture are not permanent here either. We are in danger as pilgrims in this world. This is not our final place. Do not drive your roots down too deep here; we are leaving at the end of our day.

We Americans are very rich, compared to the average person in other countries, or compared to people in the days of Jesus in the Holy Land. By those standards, almost all of us would count as rich people. We live in luxury and ease. We revel in our luxury. This concerns me because I know some Christians are going to leave lots of money and wealth here for the man of sin to use against Jesus in the time of tribulation. The Apostle James put it this way in James 5:3, " . . . Ye have heaped treasure together for the last days."

Dr Avery Rogers told me that when Colonel Sanders, the founder of Kentucky Fried Chicken was saved in the early 1970's, he sold the franchise rights for two million dollars. His income tax lawyer said, "Now, Mr. Sanders, when you die, the government gets 90 percent of this." That is what they got in those days. He sat there in awe. Then he said, "I have been a lost sinner through the years (he was saved when he was 80 years old) let's give it in the name of Jesus. Jesus is going to get this. I will not let the devil's crowd have it." They will get it if you do not give it to the work of Jesus.

We think we are fixed up here forever, but we are not going to stay here. Sheep were very busy searching for a permanent place. They did not stay in the fold very long. They were traveling. They were pilgrims. From day one, they were pilgrims being directed. They were not just wandering around. They had a pilgrimage to perform. They had to be going where the shepherd led, doing what the shepherd directed. They were on a directed pilgrimage, with everyone under the control of the shepherd. We are not in God's flock to run around on our own, like so many people try to do today. We are on a divinely appointed pilgrimage, every one of us that is part of the Great Shepherd's flock.

So I will use this term pilgrims, in this chapter. You understand, I am referring to the sheep when I use it. I want to point out the tools concerning your pilgrimage to your final abode.

1. The pilgrim's Attendants. First of all, the pilgrims have some things that attend them. You are being attended, the scripture says, and here are your attendants: "Surely, goodness and mercy shall follow me all the days of my life." Goodness and mercy are your attendants. These attendants were taken from the shepherd's knowledge of the sheep dog. The book of Job talks about having sheep dogs. Job 30:1 says, "...whose fathers I would have disdained to have set with the dogs of

my flock." The shepherd, if he was able, sometimes owned two dogs, trained in how to control sheep. The shepherd led, the dogs brought up the rear. They followed the sheep. That is why David says, "goodness and mercy shall follow me." They follow the sheep.

His shepherd dogs followed, and the shepherd never had to worry about the sheep in back. Everything was quiet. The shepherd knew the dogs were keeping the sheep in line. If a proud sheep started to stray, a dog would bring it back. They might have to resort to a nip on the leg, to make it get in line, but it worked. His dogs were not in the very middle. They kept following them in a file line. A shepherd's dog followed them and sometimes was beside them to protect them. The sheep would know that the dog had the authority of the shepherd.

Sometimes a man could not afford to have dogs. He did not own dogs. Then he took his sling, and if the sheep started to stray, he would put a rock in the sling and throw it over that sheep to startle it. Sometimes it would run past the line. Then he would throw a rock on that side and get him back in line. The two rocks were meant to hound the sheep, like goodness and mercy. It is the sheep in Psalm 23 that is saying, "goodness and mercy shall follow me." You know what that means? Follow is from the same Hebrew root word as "hunt." That reminds me of hunting with hounds, so the sheep could be saying, "Goodness and mercy are hounding me, just right on my heels."

This is exactly what happens. Goodness and mercy keep the sheep in line. You know what goodness and mercy are. Goodness refers to God in His provision, His compassion, His grace and His love. All of that is included in the goodness of God. That really means His provisions for you. He is good enough to find everything you will need in the pilgrim's walk. The Shepherd's goodness is His love and His grace provided for you. Another word for mercy is pity. Mercy will get you through a problem brought on for whatever reason, including your own sin. God is just being merciful, that's all. That's the only reason He would have done it; he is just merciful. Mercy is filled with pity and a willingness to forgive. It includes pardon.

When a sheep starts going astray, he needs the mercy of the shepherd. If the shepherd did not have mercy, the sheep would probably lose its life. It had to have mercy, mercy when it strayed. You need that every day of your life. People who think they do not need mercy do not know the Lord. Any time we do not have mercy, we need it. It is God's, the Great Shepherd's goodness and mercy, provided by His grace, that we must have to get all the way home. Those are our attendants. I like them. I like my sheepdogs. I am glad they are taking care of me. I need them every day. Jesus said, "I will not leave you," and "Lo I am with you always." To which the sheep confidently and joyously reply, "all the days of my life."

2. The pilgrim's Affirmation. Notice what the sheep says: "surely." Without a doubt, it affirms it. It is affirming an absolute certainty. Surely, like, amen, amen, an affirmation. I love that word "surely." It is an absolute certainty that you will complete the pilgrimage. In I John 4:13 we find, "Hereby know we that we dwell in him, and he in us, because he hath given us of his Spirit." Again, in I John 5:11-13, "And this is the record, that God hath given us eternal life, and this life is in his Son. He that hath the Son, hath life; and he that hath not the Son of God hath not life. These things have I written unto you that believe on the name of the Son of God; that ye may know that ye have eternal life, and that ye may believe on the name of the Son of God." Paul said in II Timothy 1:12, " . . . I know whom I have believed, and am persuaded that he is able to keep that which I have committed unto him against that day."

These are emphatic statements of faith. The sheep affirms that the dogs are going to follow it all the days of its life. It said "all the days of my life." Everything in Psalm 23 from the very first reference to the Lord, my Shepherd winds up in these words, "all the days of my life." Every day those sheepdogs are out all day long, not quitting. All day long they are with you, all the days of your life. That's a great feeling. Rest assured that a pilgrim is all right, without doubt.

The sheep was expressing and affirming its faith and its confidence. Knowing that we have a pilgrimage, that affirmation from that sheep tells us everything. "Surely" it will turn out all right. As sheep we have two faithful dogs, goodness and mercy, all the days of our lives.

3. The pilgrim's Anticipation. Hear what the sheep says. "I will dwell in the house of the Lord forever." The sheep was not there when it said this. It was on the journey .It was anticipating. It was looking forward to it. That is where the pilgrim is to live. You are to look forward to it. Abraham did not have a home or a city, "For he looked for a city which hath foundations, whose builder and maker is God" (Hebrews 11:10). He looked for one. We are to live in anticipation of the Lord's house.

What you really need to do is live in anticipation of the coming of Jesus to carry you there. You are to anticipate His coming to carry you to your eternal home. We ought to live in daily anticipation. If you do not live in daily anticipation, you will go wandering off. If you are not living in daily expectation and anticipation of the coming of the Lord Jesus Christ to carry you home, you may be like the evil servant in Matthew 24:48 that said, " . . . My Lord delayeth his coming," and went about getting drunk and taking advantage of his master's absence. When you have lost your anticipation of Jesus coming to carry you to an eternal home, you're in bad shape. We are to live in anticipation of His coming to carry us to that eternal fold. Whenever a person lives looking forward to the Lord's coming it indicates that he does not have an abiding home here.
Abraham did not have an abiding home here. He was a stranger here, the scripture says. He did not have one, but he looked for a particular one. He was living in anticipation. Abraham was a

stranger in the land of Canaanites. Hebrews never called the place they lived home. It was not their home. It was a fold, temporary. They did not call the house they lived in a home. We westerners do. We call everything home, starting with home plate. There are folks that build houses, but lots of them are not homebuilders. You do not build a home that way, just because you have a house. There are lots of houses that do not have a home in them. It takes something different. You might have a fold here, but that is not your permanent home; you will leave that thing someday. You live in a house that is called a tabernacle, your body. You live in one that is going to decay and fall down. This is not where you are going to stay. You are just passing through. Live in anticipation of the final home. One way I knew I am saved is that I have an affinity for heaven.

The Apostle Paul said of himself " . . . having a desire to depart, and be with Christ; which is far better" (Philippians 1:23). I do not know how anyone can say they know the Lord if they have no affinity for the Lord's house. When I was lost, I did not have any affinity for heaven. There was not anything there I was interested in. But now, I have anticipation about it. By the way, I know a lot who are over there now. Jesus, Paul, Avery Rogers, Alice Moore, father, mother, father-in-law, mother-in-law, three brothers, one sister, and all the saints from Abel until now. They are part of that that great crowd of witnesses Paul wrote about. That is something
to look forward to with great anticipation.

If you are in Him, you are looking forward to being with Him in the eternal home. That is the pilgrim's anticipation.

4. The pilgrim's Assurance. The sheep said I "will dwell" in the house of the Lord. No question about it. The sheep is assured of it. It really knew that. There are some things that gave the sheep that assurance. The sheep knew the guidance on its pilgrimage by the shepherd, and the provisions the shepherd made for it. All that made it sure. There was not anything uncertain about those things.

The shepherd's guidance and the provisions of the shepherd are the basis of its assurance. The provisions of the shepherd, the power of the shepherd, the passion of the shepherd, the presence of the shepherd, and the presence of the two sheepdogs. No question about it. The sheep could say to itself, I am going to get there. It lived in assurance; it lived in assurance of faith. It believed it would happen; it was assured of it. You will never be assured, apart from faith. The sheep had faith in the shepherd, and in everything he did. The sheep had faith in the shepherd's dogs that guarded it and followed it all the days of its life. That faith was made a living thing, and its assurance was not something mechanical.

Faith will give assurance to you, if you know the Shepherd like you should. Paul wrote in Romans 8:25, " But if we hope for that we see not, then do we with patience wait for it." Jesus said in John 14:1-3, "Let not your heart be troubled: Ye believe in God, believe also in me. In my Father's house are many mansions: if it were not so, I would have told you. I go to prepare a place for you. And if I go and prepare a place for you, I will come again, and receive you unto myself; that where I am there ye may be also." In the continuation of this discourse of Jesus in John 14, not only did He promise He would come again, but He said He would leave us His peace (verse27) and would send the Comforter to us (verse26).

5. The pilgrim's Arrival. The sheep did arrive. The shepherd took his sheep out in the early morning, he fed them, he watered them, he guided them, he brought them to the fold. Sometimes, though, the weather conditions became so bad that the sheep could not stay in the open range any longer. The shepherd then turned them toward his house, his home, where he lived. He had a place there for them, every one of them, in the house. He built his house over where the sheep stayed. The shepherd would take them to that house. Did you know the sheep knew when they had arrived? They would gallop and they would jump around. They would swoop their tails. They

knew they had arrived. They liked it. They were back in the house.

That sheep had a home that had been built by the hands of the shepherd. It was not just a temporary fold; it was permanent. Their arrival day was a very, very important day. The shepherd's wife and children who stayed at home were there. They were glad for them to come. Those kids liked some of those lambs and petted them. By the way, you know when they were going to have to sacrifice for their sins, the Passover lamb had to be put in the house and stay 14 days with the kids and family. It ate with them. It got to be precious to them. They hated to see it killed. It was real precious.

There is going to be an arrival day at the eternal fold. It is certainly going to be a day of jubilation. There is going to be a great shout. Even the angels are going to be rejoicing in our presence. We are sure to get there, to be part of the pilgrims' arrival. That day of arrival is coming. Those sheep got back to the shepherd's house for sure. On a given day, they arrived. So you are going to arrive if you are a child of God. If you are a member the flock, He is going to guide you until you do arrive. The dogs are going to keep on your trail. I sometimes call them the hounds of heaven. They are right on you. That is why the sheep says, "I will dwell in the house of the Lord forever."

6. The pilgrim's Abode. The sheep say, "the house of the Lord." Not the one you built, but the one He has built for you.A. Look at the nature of that abode for a moment. It is the Lord's house. Jesus said in John 14:2&3, "In my Father's house are many mansions . . . I go to prepare a place for you. And if I go and prepare a place for you, I will come again, and receive you unto myself; that where I am, there ye may be also."

Some scholars say that is one of the strongest statements in the Bible. "In my Father's house are many mansions." When he was a boy, Samuel the prophet had a fleece. He slept on it in the house of

God, where Eli the high priest was. What this says in terms a sheep can understand is, in my Father's house are many fleeces - one for everybody, one for each of you. It means it is wonderful. It is the Lord's house. It is not a house built with hands. It belongs to Him. He is going to take you there to His house.

Back in Palestine when a young man married, he did not run off someplace else. You know what they did? They just added some more onto the house. They built it in court fashion. They all lived there as a family, together. Each one had a flock of sheep and there was a place provided for them in each section. It was like the Father's house, the Lord's house.

A.   It is a permanent abode; it is forever. The sheep who lives there will never have to journey any more, never have to climb over hot, hard rocks and be chased by the vipers and other enemies. It is there forever. "I will dwell in the house of the Lord forever." Nothing here on earth can last forever. It all vanishes, it all leaves. Nothing down here is going to last. God is going to burn this thing off some day, but we will have one eternal home, the Lord's house, that lasts forever.

B.   It is a provident house. There will not be a thing there that you dislike. It is going to be perfection. You will never get thirsty again, never get hungry again, never have to face any need. Everything you need is completely provided. That is what the Good Shepherd meant when he said, "I go to prepare." He was a shepherd. He prepared the tableland. He prepared everything for the sheep. He is preparing that abode for you. He is making it ready. He is there, making it ready. He is furnishing everything in it that anybody could ever need or want, and that is for all eternity. That is a glorious place. You will have lots of good friends up there, and live in the presence of the Shepherd, where you can actually look right upon His face. You will be with Him. There is going to be rest for the weary. There are all kind of provisions; all your hopes will be revived. There will not be a thing you ever hoped for that will not be met. It is the Lord's house. It is the new Jerusalem, described in Revelation, Chapters 21 and 22. It is a thoroughly furnished home for the sheep of God's pasture.

I want to leave with you the Shepherd's benediction and blessing, from Hebrews 13:20&21:

"Now the God of peace, that brought again from the dead our Lord Jesus, that Great Shepherd of the sheep, through the blood of the everlasting covenant, Make you perfect in every good work to do his will, working in you that which is well-pleasing in his sight, through Jesus Christ; to whom be the glory for ever and ever". "AMEN".

Bibliography

Adams, J. Mckee, Biblical Backgrounds (Broadman, 1965)

Edersheim, Alfred, the life and Times of Jesus the Messiah, 2 Vol. (Longmans 1896)

Harris, R. Laird, Man God's eternal Creation (Moody, 1971)

Hutcheson, George, An Exposition of John's Gospel (Sovereign Grace Publishers)

Laird, Harold Samuel, Portraits of Christ in the Gospel of John (The Bible Institute Colportage Assn.)

Lockridge, S. M., Messages on Evangelism (Daniel's Publishers, 1970)

Morris, Leon, Commentary on the Gospel of John (Erdmans, 1971)

Pink, Arthur W., The Attributes of God (Reiner)

Rogers, Avery, The Shepherd and His Sheep (unpublished lectures recorded 1974 by author)

Ruckman, Peter, S., The Book of Job (Pensecola Bible Press 1998)

Ruckman, Peter, S., The Book of Revelation (Pensecola Bible Press, 1970)

Ruckman, Peter, S., The Gospel of Matthew (Pensecola Bible Press, 1970)

Ruckman, Peter, S., The Sure Word of Prophecy (Pensecola Bible Press, 1996)

Ruckman, Peter, S., The Book of Genesis (Pensecola Bible Press, 1969)

Spurgeon, C. H., The Treasury of David, 3 Vol, (Zondervan, 1966)

Stone, J. Nathan, Names of God (Moody, 1944)

Strong, Augustus H., Systematic Theology (Judson, 1907)

Stevens, William Wilson, Doctrines of the Christian Religion (Eerdmans, 1967)

Unger, Merrill F. Archeology and the New Testament (Zondervan, 1962)

Watts, J. Wash, Old Testament Teaching (Broadman, 1967)

Wright, Fred H., Manners and Customs of the Bible Lands (Moody, 1953)

Yates, Kylem, Study in Psalms (Broadman, 1953)

Dr. Lee is available for speaking engagements and personal appearances. For more information contact:

Dr. Frankie Lee
C/O Advantage Books
P.O. Box 160847
Altamonte Springs, Florida   32716

To purchase additional copies of this book or other books published by Advantage Books call our toll free order number at:
1-888-383-3110 (Book Orders Only)

or visit our bookstore website at:
www.advbookstore.com

Longwood, Florida, USA
"we bring dreams to life"™
www.advbooks.com

Printed in the United States
136301LV00001B/4/P